Shropshire in the Civil War

Terry Bracher and Roger Emmett

D1575090

To Bill

Best wishes

from

Roger Emmett

Shropshire
Books

Front cover: Charles I addressing loyal Shropshire
gentry at Gay Meadow, Shrewsbury, 1642

Back cover: Hopton Castle. Photo: Gordon Dickins

ISBN: 0-903802-78-3

Cover and Book Design: The Graphic Terrace
Managing Editor: Helen Sample

Published by Shropshire Books, the publishing
imprint of Shropshire County Council's
Community and Environment Services Directorate

Printed in Great Britain by Livesey Limited

About the Authors

Roger Emmett has lived in Shropshire for twenty years and teaches History in Staffordshire.

Terry Bracher was a librarian at Shropshire Records & Research Centre and is now Local Studies Librarian for Northamptonshire.

Acknowledgements

The authors are indebted to Helen Sample who helped turn our rather heavy text into a readable book.

We would like to thank the following for permission to reproduce illustrations:

David Brierley, p 90.
Gordon Dickins, pp 9-12, 15, 16, 49, 50-54, 56, 92, 94-96.
Kathryn Green, *vii*.
Bridgnorth Borough Council (Prince Rupert's letter), p 75.
Leominster Library (Brampton Bryan), p 67.
Edward Harley Esquire (Lady Brilliana Harley), p 68.
Bodleian Library, University of Oxford (Enoch ap Evan murders, Bodleian shelfmark, Wood 365(7)), p 17.
Countess of Sutherland (Wem estate map), p 89.
Charlesworth & Valentine, p. 93.
Shropshire Records and Research for all other illustrations.

Few books on any aspect of Shropshire's history would ever make it to print without the considerable assistance of Tony Carr, and this monograph is no exception. Thanks are also due to Mary McKenzie, David Portch and all the staff at Shropshire Records & Research, who continue to provide a service second to none.

George Baugh and David Cox of the V.C.H. always gave their time generously when helping us to solve mysterious references, while Bill Champion, Barbara Coulton and Peter Francis-Wemys pointed us towards some important sources.

This book also could not have progressed without the invaluable help of Janet Saffron, who read and corrected our drafts. However, any errors in the text are solely the responsibility of the authors.

There are many people, though they may not have realised it, who gave us encouragement when it was needed.

They include: John Moore, Wayne Richards, Billy Cooper, John Box, Steve Wright, Dimitrios Koutsohionis, Paul & Jo Mitchell, Lynn Stoddart, Dave Griffiths, Margaret Davies, Peter & Maggie Stevens, Roger & Linda Pritchard, Carolyn Lester, Yiannis Christakos,

Brian Gregory, Bryan Quy, Ray Dench, Beryl & Peter Davies, Doris Bracher, Gary Bracher, Donald Carter and Ella Henderson.

Finally, to Judy and Julia: All we can promise is a moratorium on any more histories of the Civil War!

Contents

A map of Shropshire in the early seventeenth century

Introduction

In 1625 Charles I came to the throne and was soon involved in arguments with Parliament regarding finance and religion. More extreme in his religious views than his father, James I, Charles determined to rule without Parliament. By using a series of highly unpopular methods of taxation, he managed to govern successfully for several years.

Charles' attempt to introduce the English prayer book into Scotland in 1637 involved him in a disastrous war, so that by 1640 he was forced to recall Parliament. Full of dissatisfaction, the Puritan gentry that made up the Long Parliament of 1640, clashed with Charles during the following two years, until the deep mistrust of each other's religious and political motives could not be resolved other than by war.

Although there were no major battles in Shropshire, the war was bloody and had a far-reaching effect upon its population. The history of the war in Shropshire in a sense reflects the conduct of the war nationally, as one of attrition that eventually ended in the King's defeat.

By 1649, the King had been executed, the House of Lords abolished, and a republic established in what became known as the 'English Revolution'.

Bloody Designs
Shropshire Goes to War

In 1642 King Charles I addressed his subjects in the market place in Shrewsbury:

> "Be not afraid, I would to God my poor Subjects suffered no more by the Insolence and Violence of that Army raised against me (though they have made themselves wanton even with Plenty) than you shall do by mine; and yet I fear I cannot prevent all Disorders. I will do my best; and this I'll promise you, no Man shall be loser by me, if I can help it."

Why did people choose to fight for or against the King in Shropshire? Shropshire was a wealthy county in terms of its agriculture and market town economy. The majority of people, therefore, were reluctant to oppose the King. Even if they disagreed with certain aspects of Charles' rule, they were unlikely to take up arms unless they had very good reasons. This reluctance can be seen in local opposition to Ship Money, one of the taxes levied by Charles before the war.

Ship Money was first introduced to inland towns in 1635. Shrewsbury was expected to pay £456 10s. This was a high sum in comparison with other towns in Shropshire and outside. John Trench, a sergeant-at-mace, complained that in attempting to collect Ship Money he received "scandalous, opprobrious and threatening speeches". However, despite this opposition the money was in the main collected, because Shropshire remained loyal to the King.

The disapproval of the tax mirrors a national experience of the gradual breakdown of royal authority between 1636-1640 during Charles' disastrous Scottish wars.

Religious Divides

There was a growing disenchantment with Charles' government, but economic motivation alone was not sufficient cause for rebellion. By far the biggest reason in Shropshire for opposing the King and taking up arms against him was religion. During the 1630s,

Fruitful the Land

In 1627, John Speed described Shropshire:

"The soile is rich, and standeth most upon a reddish clay, abounding in wheat and barley, pit coales, iron, and woods; which two last continue not long in league together. It hath Rivers that make fruitfull the Land, and in their waters containe great store of fresh-fish, whereof Severne is the chiefe, and second in the Realme, whose streame cutteth this County in the middest, and with many windings sporteth her selfe forward, leaving both pastures and meadowes bedecked with flowers and greene colours, which every where shee bestoweth upon such her attendants."

In the early seventeenth century most people earned their living through agriculture or trades associated with it. Farming varied throughout the county depending on the geography, but most farmers' capital was invested in livestock. Cattle were reared everywhere, but particularly in the north of the county where dairying was more common. Sheep were found in the hills to the south-west and the heathlands. Pig rearing had also become more frequent during this period. For many farmers the fattening of pigs was a safe way of making money in addition to their traditional forms of stock rearing.

Horses were essential to the majority of farms which would have a variety of animals to suit different tasks - packhorses being the commonest - and the larger landowners bred horses. On his death in 1665, Sir Walter Acton of Aldenham left a total of 23 horses valued at £122 3s. 4d.

All farmers kept poultry, and had other means of supplementing income and diet included bee keeping and goat breeding. Small game provided an opportunity for poaching, as did fishing, though many people had free access to ponds and rivers.

Although most Shropshire farmers made the bulk of their living through livestock management, arable farming had also increased. Wherever possible farmers diversified and mixed farming was becoming widespread. More land was also being brought under cultivation and used for grazing. The process of enclosure - that is the organisation of farmland into compact holdings - was well underway during the seventeenth century.

The clearing of woods and the drainage of wetlands were the most significant activities in increasing the area of farmland. The wetland area of the Weald Moors in the east of the county saw the largest reclamation of land and by 1650, 2,730 acres in the area around Wrockwardine had been enclosed.

More land was cultivated because the population steadily increased in the early seventeenth century and there was an expanding market for food. Between 1563 and 1672 it is estimated that the population of the county increased by 64%. Farmers could increase their income if they grew more corn or raised more animals. New opportunities arose and the ownership of land underwent significant change during this period. More people owned land. Families that had made money, for example in commerce and the law, invested in land to improve their social standing and sought to maximise their investment. The Shrewsbury mercer, Thomas Ireland, invested part of his wealth in land throughout the county, such as at Albrighton Heath.

Landowners, both new and old, were intent on exploiting the mineral resources on their estates. In 1610, a sale of several manors near Gretton between the Lacon family and Isaac Jones, a merchant tailor and Richard Newell, a draper, both from London, included "fishing places, mines and quarries". On the eve of the Civil War, Sir Vincent Corbet possessed "colemynes" and "colepitts" as part of the manor of Lawley. Other early industrial activity included iron making. There were numerous sites in the county, including Leighton, Bouldon and Sir Basil Brooke's new furnance at Coalbrookdale.

The changing patterns of land ownership indicate an increased social mobility, and although it was the gentry who benefited most, many smaller farmers also prospered. The number of yeomen (farmers owning their own land) seems to have increased and, in comparison with other more eastern arable counties, Shropshire seems to have been prosperous without the extremes of wealth and poverty apparent elsewhere.

the Puritans believed that the King was the victim of a popish plot to return the country to Catholicism. They were convinced that Charles was surrounded by evil advisors and Parliament was thus a vital means of curbing dangerous influences on the King.

Early seventeenth century minds still wanted everyone to belong to the same church. During the reign of Elizabeth I the Church of England became firmly established, but not without argument as to theology and practice, and divisions began to emerge within its ranks. Some people left the church to become recusants, that is those who refused to attend the services of the Church of England. They were liable to fines for non-attendance. An example were the Puritan Baptists who believed in spiritual regeneration through adult baptism. They had their own places of worship, such as the Baptist meeting house in Golden Cross Passage, Shrewsbury, established in 1628.

The largest groups of recusants, however, were Catholics, who still retained their faith despite the fines imposed on them. Their services were held in private chapels, usually in large houses belonging to local Catholic gentry. In addition to the secret chapels, these buildings also contained hiding places for visiting priests. Both can be found at Boscobel House and Plowden Hall, owned by the Giffards and the Plowdens. It was the support of such families, which ensured the survival of Catholicism in England.

Some were open about their Catholicism, such as the Brooke family of Madeley Court. Sir Basil Brooke was treasurer of the Catholic Queen Henrietta's household as well as a notable local leader. However, being openly Catholic could be dangerous, as in the case of Edward Lloyd of Llwyny-Maen, near Oswestry. It was reported that Lloyd had expressed "uncontained joy" at the news of the defeat of the King's son in law, Frederick, the Protestant Elector Palatine in Bohemia. This was followed by a heated debate in Parliament where the Members were determined to punish his actions. The King referred the matter to the House of Lords who promptly sentenced Lloyd to "pillory, branding, fine and degradation from the status of a gentleman".

Others were far more clandestine about their beliefs. Sir Francis Ottley of Pitchford served as a JP, yet was widely thought to be a Catholic. Notably, his house, Pitchford Hall, contained several priest holes and a private chapel.

Sir Basil Brooke, a prominent Catholic and member of the local gentry

The Church kept records of recusants. In particular Archbishop Laud's Visitation of 1635 lists around two hundred Catholics living in parishes within the Deaneries of Shrewsbury and Bridgnorth. Of those who were listed, many appeared to cluster around the homes of Catholic landowners, who preferred to employ those who were of the same faith. The Giffards, for example, employed the Penderel family at Boscobel House, while the largest Catholic community in the county centred on the Brooke estates in Madeley. During the reign of James I the Church of England began to display obvious divisions. There were many people who believed that the reforms of the Protestant church had not gone far enough. In Scotland the church had a Calvinistic flavour; there were no bishops and church elders assumed greater influence in its administration. Many English worshippers believed that the church should be reformed on similar lines. Others favoured leaving things as they were or increasing state control. Thus a tension developed within the English church. Those who believed in further reform came to be known as Puritans.

Many examples of minor discord exist in local records. For instance, in 1605 five burgesses of Ludlow, including Richard Bailey and Edward Crowther, were charged with wearing their hats during divine service.

Puritans had an extremely devout, Calvinistic, approach to religion. They believed in predestination and that they were part of an elect body of souls chosen by God to enter the kingdom of Heaven. Their strict lifestyle advertised this fact.

Richard Baxter described the distinctiveness of being Puritan within the local community of Eaton Constantine where local people enjoyed dancing around a maypole and playing music:

> "Many times my mind was inclined to be among them, and sometimes I broke loose from conscience and joined with them; and the more I did it, the more I was inclined to do it. But when I heard them call my father Puritan, it did much to cure me; for I considered that my father's exercise of reading the Scriptures was much better than theirs."

Whilst these disagreements existed during James' reign, the church did largely remain unified, although because of religious persecution some Puritans left England, notably the Pilgrim Fathers in 1620 (including some of the More family to whom a plaque remains in Shipton church). During Charles reign, however, these rifts increased and became gaping chasms as the crown clearly favoured the ideas of Arminius, the Dutch theologian. He advocated that the church should be organised as a hierarchical structure with bishops and lesser clergy in charge of biblical interpretation. More importantly, Arminians were opposed to the concept of predestination, believing instead in the idea of 'free will' – that entry to heaven depended on one's actions in life rather than being one of the elect. Theologically this still encompassed the Protestant faith, but Puritans believed it represented a return towards Catholicsm. Puritans had little doubt that Arminians were really closet Catholics. Therefore, when Charles appointed the Arminian William Laud Archbishop of Canterbury and his reforms began to be introduced throughout Shropshire, Puritans were alarmed.

The Power of the Church

During the seventeenth century the church could not be separated from the state and society. It represented authority and stability, law and order. In many cases it was the only outlet for news and, occasionally, propaganda. The church was also the regulator of moral behaviour. The extent of its power can be seen in the way it pervaded everyday life. In 1638 court records for the Archdeaconry of Ludlow show that Richard Titherland of Westbury was excommunicated for profaning the Sabbath by "playing at tabor and pipe" and encouraging "divers to profane the Sabbath by dancing at unlawful times." The penalty of excommunication from the church was commonly used to punish moral offenders. In 1612 Francisca Fletcher of Ditton Priors suffered this fate when "she reported herself to be with childe by Jon Holland senior and was delivered in his house", as did Daniell Baker, a silk weaver from Kinlet, because "he abused Mr Harte with unseemlie words and called him knave".

The threat of such sanctions carried far greater weight than it would today. Johannis Smaleman of Ditton Priors was censured "for keeping companie with excommunicate persons". Despite this, some people still refused to be intimidated by the church's power. In 1619 Edmund Leigh of Ludlow, in abusing the rector, shouted: "Go, goose-cap fool. A fart for you!"

The church was also economically powerful. Despite the reformation, the church as an institution was still a wealthy landowner and this wealth continued to be built upon the collection of tithes. Payments of tithes to Thomas Habberly the vicar of Diddlebury in 1637 demonstrate that most inhabitants in the parish were required to pay this tax. It included "the tithes of all corn and grain growing and increasing in the villages or hamlets of Corfton and Sparchford". No stone was left unturned. "The tithe milk of every cow kept in the parish" fetched "one penny" and "there are due to the vicar all other small tithes as wool, lambs, apples, pears, and other fruite, geese, piggs, hemp and flax".

The symbolic separation of the altar from the congregation by an altar rail emphasised the importance of the clergyman as being the sole interpreter of the scriptures. It emphasised the Communion and thus seemed to many to be an attempt to pave the way for a return to the Catholic Mass. Laud was totally opposed to the Calvinist concept of a congregation that debated the Bible. He saw such practices not only as blasphemy, but socially disruptive. Laud thought Puritans to be subversive. They challenged the authority of the king and the stability of a structured and ordered society. Where might such people power end? The Laudian rituals and artefacts, therefore, symbolised an ideological struggle that also had political overtones.

Richard Baxter

B.1615 d.1691. Richard Baxter was one of the foremost Puritans of his time. Born in Rowton, Shropshire, his early life was spent in Eaton Constantine. His father was a reformed gambler who became a Puritan. This had great influence upon the young Baxter. He despaired of the local clergy, some of whom were his teachers, perceiving them to be "ignorant and immoral" men. Baxter eventually attended the free endowed school at Wroxeter and on his master's advice moved to the Royal Court at Ludlow and then to the Royal Court in London. A courtier's life was not fulfilling and he moved back to Eaton Constantine at the earliest opportunity. During the illness of his former master John Owen, he was persuaded to teach at the school in Wroxeter. It was not until after the death of his mother that Baxter seriously considered a career in the church under the Rev Francis Garbet of Wroxeter.

In his early twenties, Baxter became friendly with two notable nonconformists, Walter Craddock and Joseph Symonds, and attended their meetings in Shrewsbury. While he disagreed with their doctrines, it was the persecution of such friends by the established church that eventually led him to oppose the Laudian reforms.

In 1638 Baxter was ordained and offered the position of headmaster at an endowed school in Dudley. In this town he again befriended nonconformists. Baxter's own beliefs were unclear. He disliked wearing the surplice and opposed the cross in baptism, yet he saw nothing wrong with bishops and the liturgy. By 1640, while holding a position at Bridgnorth, he had rejected the Laudian oath that sought to bind clergy to episcopacy and Arminian theology.

In 1641 a committee of the parish of Kidderminster asked Baxter to take up the position of lecturer. Within two years he had apparently transformed the parish into a godly community. When war finally came, Baxter's growing disenchantment with the Church of England led him to take sides with Parliament.

Having to flee from Kidderminster, Baxter joined various Parliamentary garrisons. In 1643 Humphrey Mackworth and Thomas Hunt asked him to join them at Wem in the anticipation that this would also encourage some of his supporters to follow. He stayed for just two weeks, during which time he managed to negotiate the release of his father from the Royalist garrison at Lilleshall, before returning to the main Parliamentary garrison at Coventry.

After the Civil War Baxter returned to Kidderminster and wrote a series of religious works. His politics upset many people. While generally agreeing with the idea of the Commonwealth, he disliked Cromwell and found himself supporting the restoration of the monarchy. However, while living in London during the reigns of Charles II and James II, the establishment considered him a nonconformist. Refusing to sign the Act of Uniformity in 1662, he began preaching in meeting houses. In May 1685 he was tried by Judge Jeffreys, fined and imprisoned for over a year and a half. Still active in 1688, he entered a "coalition of Protestant dissenters" against the Catholicism of James II. He survived into the reign of William and Mary, and died on 8th December 1691.

Baxter's fame rests upon the sheer volume of writing he produced during his life. His works reflect the importance of religious thought in the minds of ordinary people, and provide an insight into the debates and disputes of seventeenth century religion.

Richard Baxter (1615-91) an eminent Puritan

George Lawson

B. c.1598 d.1678. Little is known of George Lawson's early life. He was probably born in the parish of Giggleswick in Yorkshire and educated at Cambridge University. Lawson came to Shropshire around 1636 when he obtained a position as a salaried clergyman in Mainstone and received a licence to preach from Archbishop Laud on 22nd June of the same year.

Lawson is interesting because of his unwillingness to conform to either Puritan or Laudian ideals, which has led some historians to portray him as an archetypal 'Vicar of Bray'. However, this image is inaccurate. As a young and very able scholar he fulfilled the criteria of higher educational standards set out by Laud for aspiring clergymen, yet he also appeared acceptable to Puritans. He was involved in the controversy over the Enoch Ap Evan axe murders, helping Richard More to frame the rejection of the conspiracy theory put forward by Peter Studley in "The Looking Glasse of Schism" (1635).

The Puritan lawyer, Humphrey Mackworth, then tried to help him secure a living at St. Chad's in Shrewsbury by portraying him as an Arminian so that he would be acceptable to Laud. This seems to have worked as Laud tried to impose Lawson upon the parish of St. Chad's in 1637 as curate and preacher. This overturned the popular choice of the parishioners who had elected Richard Poole, a Calvinist of apparently lesser intellect. Amid a climate of growing resistance to Government policy, the parishioners rejected the royal directive and Lawson failed to secure his living. Lawson was then offered a position in the parish of More by its patron Richard More of Linley, where he remained until his death in 1678.

In truth Lawson's theology fell between the extremes of Puritanism and Arminianism. He managed to remain in his living throughout the Civil War. By 1660 he completed a major work in political philosophy and theology entitled Politica Sacra et Civilis, and it is for this he is remembered. He argued that the individual had a loyalty to God and the community above hierarchical institutions. Yet at the same time he advocated a unified church that was pragmatic in relating to the community it served. He argued for a consensus approach to religious and political matters. Whilst government was necessary, there was no such thing as an "ideal" government. Lawson stated that what mattered at the time was not the search for a perfect order, on which there was bound to be great argument, but some order framed by consensus. He wrote, "Where we cannot do what we will, we must do what we can". Published in 1660, the book was seen as being influential in helping to pave the way for the restoration of Charles II and the evolution of a constitutional monarchy with limited powers.

In Wroxeter church the altar rail is a lasting example of one of Laud's reforms, and other Arminian relics of this period also remain such as the huge candlestick holders in the church at Lydbury North. Richard Gough recalled of Myddle Church that "At that time there was a new Communion Table made, a very good one, and also new Communion Railes, which were placed square on three sides of the Communion Table". However, some churches remained unchanged. The superbly preserved Langley Chapel is an example of an Elizabethan church remarkable for its simplicity and lack of decoration.

The gruesome axe murders committed near Clun by Enoch ap Evan show the increasingly bitter divisions that ran below the surface in the local communities concerning religion, and also the eagerness to exploit any such incident for political gain by rival religious factions.

The murders took place in 1633 when Enoch ap Evan came home to his house in Clun after work in the fields and cut off his brother John's head with an axe. He then similarly killed his seventy-year-old mother. Evan claimed he had fallen out with his brother and mother over the issue of kneeling to receive communion. Peter Studley, the vicar of St Chad's, wrote a pamphlet which argued that ap Evan's Puritanism had caused him to commit the murder. Studley questioned ap Evan in prison, obsessed by the notion that Puritan dogma had unhinged the boy's mind. After he was hanged at Shrewsbury in August, his body was hung on a gibbet near his home, but was secretly taken down and buried during the middle of the night by persons unknown (later revealed to be his sister and her companions). Studley again interpreted this as a Puritan plot to break the law and undermine the social order.

Meanwhile, the Puritans claimed that ap Evan was not motivated by his religious beliefs, but a madman who had committed the murders in a fit of insanity. Studley certainly had his own axe to grind. He clearly resented the increasing use of lecturers within the church community who could earn as much as a local vicar. Studley remarked that these "priests teach for hire and the prophets thereof divine for money". There was a sizeable Puritan community in Shrewsbury. One of the most notable lecturers in Shrewsbury was Julines Herring who was appointed by the corporation in 1618 until Laud forced him out in 1635. William Rowley of Rowley's Mansion was instrumental in bringing him to Shrewsbury where he became in effect an alternative clergyman holding services in private houses, in the town, and as far afield as that of Margaret Bromley of Sheriffhales. His followers were often wealthy and prominent members of the community such as Rowley, Edward Jones and George Wright. In 1633 Wright with his wife and others were charged "for not bowing at the name of Jesus and refusing to communicate for the gesture's sake".

Taking sides

Both sides became increasingly estranged as the 1630s progressed and saw each other as threats. Whereas Catholics in the county had previously been known and tolerated, by 1640 Puritans were viewing them as dangerous plotters, presumably preparing for the overthrow of Parliament and a return to Catholicism under an autocratic ruler.

Politica Sacra & Civilis:
Or, A Model of
Civil and **Ecclesiastical**
GOVERNMENT.
WHEREIN,
Besides the positive Doctrine concerning
STATE and CHURCH in general,
Are debated the principal Controversies
of the TIMES concerning the
CONSTITUTION
OF THE
State and **Church**
OF
ENGLAND,
Tending to Righteousness, Truth,
and Peace.

By GEORGE LAWSON, Rector of
More in the County of Salop.

The Second Edition.

LONDON,
Printed for J. S. and are to be Sold by T. Goodwin at
the Maidenhead over against St. Dustans Church in
Fleet-street. 1689.

George Lawson's influential theological work
Politica Sacra et Civilis *prompted*
the restoration of the monarchy

A
True relation of the
Murders committed in the
Parish of Clunne in the County of
Salop by Enoch ap Evan upon the
Bodies of his Mother and Brother,
with the Cause moving
him thereunto.

Wherein is examined and refuted a cer-
taine Booke written upon the same Subject,
by P. STUDLEY, Entituled the
Looking glasse of SCHISME.

Also an Appendix in further defence of this
Relation, wherein are examined the most
material Passages added in the Second Edition
of the said LOOKING GLASSE, whereby
the Author vainely sheweth his desire to maintaine and excuse his er-
roneous Reports in the former
Edition of his Booke.

By RICHARD MORE Esquire.

Printed by Order of a Committee of the
Honourable House of Commons now Assembled in Parliament.

LONDON,
Printed by T. P. for P. Stephens & C. Meredith
at the golden Lyon in Pauls Church yard. 1641.

Frontispiece to Richard More's rebuttal
of Peter Studley's accusations over the
Enoch Ap Evan *axe-murders*

Richard Baxter's house in Eaton Constantine

Richard Baxter's house in Bridgnorth

The altar rail in Wroxeter church, a fine example of Laudian influence and reforms

Langley Chapel, a simple church little changed since the Reformation

Rowley's House, Shrewsbury: Once the home of William Rowley, a leading Puritan in the town, now housing the Borough Museum, its collections include artefacts from the Civil War

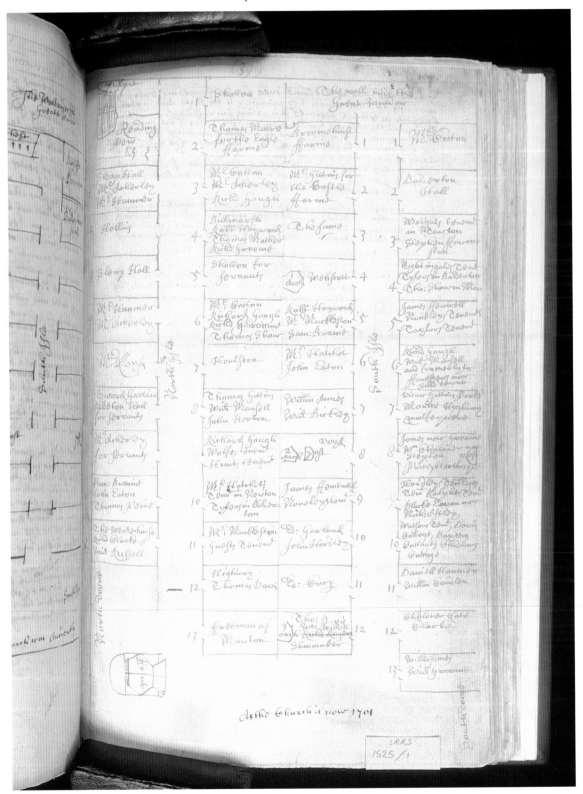

A plan of the pew arrangements in Myddle Church, which inspired Richard Gough's stories in his History of Myddle

Hopton Castle: Today's tranquil ruins belie a violent past

Albright Hussey: A sixteenth century house garrisoned by the Royalists

The notorious axe-murders performed by Enoch Ap Evan, graphically described for Peter Studley's anti-Puritan tract 'The looking Glasse of Schism'

Superstition and Witchcraft

In his history of the parish of Myddle, Richard Gough told the story of Reece Wenlocke:

> "Reece had a cow, which was stolen away, and it is reported that hee went to a woman, whom they called the wise woman of Montgomery, to know what was become of his cow; and as hee went, hee put a stone in his pocket, and told a neighbour of his that was with him that he would know whether she were a wise woman or not, by whether she knew that hee had a stone in his pockett. And it is sayd, that when hee came to her, she said, thou hast a stone in thy pocket, but it is not so big as that stone where with thou didst knock out such a neighbour's harrow tines."

Everyday life in the seventeenth century was still dominated by superstitious beliefs. Forces outside men and women's control, such as divine intervention, astrology and other signs from heaven, reinforced traditional morality. The notable antiquarian William Camden (1551-1623), believed that when an Eclipse happens in Scorpio that "'tis fatal to the Town of Shrewsbury".

However, neither Richard Gough nor William Camden makes any references to witchcraft in the county. Indeed, there appear to be few cases of witchcraft in Shropshire in the seventeenth century. In areas such as East Anglia and Lancashire, there are numerous accounts of witchcraft trials. Why should Shropshire be so different? Unfortunately, assize records do not survive for the county during the period of this study. But where records do survive there is little or no mention of witchcraft. There is some evidence to suggest that witchcraft accusations were more likely to arise in situations of economic tension, particularly where there was a high degree of poverty. Shropshire was relatively wealthy and this could explain the absence of witchcraft trials.

Yet, many Salopians did believe in witches. The Bridgnorth Corporation did not appear to find it strange that they were asked to contribute £1 4s "for the charges of condemned witches which were brought from London through this town to go into Lancashire". Court records for 1636 note a payment of "£2 for burial in Christian ground" in Shrewsbury for "Kathryn Garner, Welshwoman, found innocent of Witchcraft in Trial by Water". In 1641 there were also accusations of witchcraft against Elizabeth Conney of Castle Foregate. Within the evidence "concerning her evil behaviour" it is noted that "the said Elizabeth Conney reviled and cursed Jane Meale and wished that the said Jane might melt away like butter in the sun and not be able to cut her children bread".

In 1649, the Court in Ludlow was also presented with evidence of witchcraft. Margaret Budge of Ludlow stood accused of exorcising witchcraft, charmings and sorceries. In the examination of Margaret Jones of Richards Castle it was recorded:

> "That she heard the said Margaret Budge say that she was delivered of a child in a green meadow and there came about her many pretty things and one said that God had given her a gift to do divers things and to help them that are sick and those that have lost their goods to the knowledge of them".

It is difficult to conclude that there were no other incidences of witchcraft in Shropshire. At the very least, the evidence suggests that people in Shropshire during the seventeenth century were sufficiently superstitious to accept that it was possible for individuals to indulge in acts of witchcraft.

By the end of the year Brilliana Harley claimed that there was a "great resort of papists" at Plowden Hall "which makes some fear they have some plots". Indeed, in November 1641, the Corporation of Bridgnorth made several payments for "keeping watch", in anticipation of a "general insurrection of papists".

News of the horrors of a Catholic uprising in Ireland travelled quickly to Shropshire further fuelling such fears. On the 25th June, 1642, the House of Commons ordered the town of Shrewsbury to pay £11 8s. 2d.

to "Mr Prowde, born at Shrewsbury, but lately undone by the rebels in Ireland, and who is come to that town for relief". Nicholas Prowde had been the Archdeacon of Cassel in Ireland.

As the political crisis in London worsened during 1642 and war became imminent, people in the shires considered which side they would take if war broke out, or how they might avoid making a decision. Edward Hyde, Earl of Clarendon, remarked of Shropshire that "the number of those who desired to sit still was greater than of those who desired to engage of either party."

Lord Herbert of Chirbury

B.1583 d.1648. Edward, first Lord Herbert of Chirbury was born at Eyton-on-Severn, Shropshire, the son of Richard Herbert of Montgomery Castle. He was favoured in the courts of both Elizabeth I and James I and created a Knight of the Bath in 1603 and Sheriff of Montgomery two years later. Herbert lived a varied life, notably as a soldier and an ambassador in Europe, and counted among his friends, men of literature such as John Donne and Ben Johnson. He also had a love of duelling and was continually involved in petty quarrels. By the time he had returned to England in 1624, Herbert was in debt - largely through irregular pay - and out of favour with James I. On the accession of Charles I he petitioned the King for repayment of debts and hoped to gain a peerage, which he finally secured in 1629. In 1639 Herbert was summoned to York by the King to fight in the war with Scotland. Although reluctant to attend, pleading harassment with lawsuits and other grievances, he joined the King as requested. However, by the outbreak of the Civil War, Herbert was determined to avoid another conflict, even though his sons had joined the Royalist army.

Edward Herbert provides us with a good example of somebody who largely succeeded in remaining neutral during the Civil War. By retiring to Montgomery Castle on the Shropshire-Wales border, he hoped to sit the war out. When in February 1644 Prince Rupert requested a meeting at Shrewsbury, Herbert preferred not to court danger by associating himself with the Royalist cause and asked to be left in peace, claiming that he was able to defend his own property without the help of a garrison. He was also able to produce a couple of 'sick notes' to excuse his attendance from the war. That same month he wrote to Rupert: "Having now continued for the space of above two years in so bad a condition of health . . . I shall most humbly desire to bee excused to your Highness if I attend not your Highness in person at this time."

By 1644, after defeat at Marston Moor, Rupert was again in the vicinity and once more requested urgent help. Herbert similarly refused, saying: "Though I have the ambition to kiss your most valorous and princely hands, yet because I am newly entered into a course of physic, I do humbly desire to be excused for the present."

However, remaining neutral proved to be a difficult task. With the growing success of Parliament in Shropshire, Herbert was forced to hand over Montgomery Castle to Thomas Middleton and Colonel Mytton, but not before obtaining a reasonable settlement by recounting tales of his resistance against Prince Rupert and claiming that sickness had earlier prevented him from returning to London to deliver his castle to Parliament.

Herbert spent the rest of the war in his London abode. When hostilities ceased he outwardly supported Parliament, but effectively remained outside politics. He devoted the rest of his life to literature and died in 1648.

Edward, Lord Herbert of Chirbury (1583-1648) managed to avoid being drawn into the conflict

Parliament passed a Militia Bill in February 1642 which placed the 'Trained Bands' (citizens who could muster as troops) under their command. Charles retaliated in the summer by issuing the Commissions of Array (royal edicts authorising local gentry to raise troops). As both these legal devices for raising troops depended on the gentry to organise them, it was the nobility and gentry who were forced to make a choice. Leaders of local communities with vast powers as magistrates and landlords, their influence on local people was highly significant. While many commoners waited to see which way the wind blew, or hoped that the storm would by-pass them, those of higher rank had to decide where their loyalties lay. By and large those of high social status in Shropshire sided with the King. In August, a Grand Jury filled with Royalist gentry voted to assure the King of the county's support. Among their number were the High Sheriff Sir John Weld, Sir Paul Harris, Sir Thomas Woolrich, Sir Vincent Corbet, Sir William Owen, Edward Cresset, Thomas Eyton, Roger Kynnaston, Walter Pigott, Humphrey Billingsley and Francis Ottley.

Sir Francis Ottley was particularly active in raising troops for the King and was rewarded with a knighthood for his efforts in recruiting when Charles reached Shrewsbury in September 1642. He convinced others who wavered to side with the crown, such as Richard Newport who was one of the most influential landowners in the county. Other notable Royalists included William Blunden of Blunden Hall, Thomas Scriven of Frodesley, the Lloyds of Llanforda and the Owens of Porkington. Richard Lloyd, son of the much troubled Catholic Edward Lloyd of Llwyn-y-Maen, also joined with the King. Of the county's twelve MPs, eight supported the crown. These were Sir Richard Lee (county), Sir Robert Howard (Bishop's Castle), Thomas Whitmore (Bridgnorth), Edward Acton (Bridgnorth), Ralph Goodwyn (Ludlow), Charles Baldwin (Ludlow), Francis Newport (Shrewsbury), Thomas Littleton (Much Wenlock). For Parliament were Sir John Corbet (county), Richard More (Bishop's Castle), William Pierpoint (Much Wenlock), and William Spurstowe (Shrewsbury).

Parliamentarian gentry included Thomas Mytton of Halston, Humphrey Mackworth of Betton, Thomas Hunt of Boreatton and Robert Clive of Styche. All those in opposition were against Arminian reforms, and religion appears to have been the commonest reason for taking arms against the King. Sir Robert

Harley of Brampton Bryan, fearful of a Catholic take-over, wrote to John Aston of Ludlow in 1641, "look well to your town, for the papists are discovered to have a bloody design." By June 1642 the Harleys clearly perceived the King's cause to be a Catholic one.

Below the gentry the pressure to take sides was less marked, but similar considerations were in evidence. Puritans would obviously oppose the king, though the speed of their declaration was less rapid. Although it had yet to disclose its support for either side, the threat of war prompted the Shrewsbury Corporation to improve the town's defences. As early as October 1641, four new cannon were bought for £20, the walls repaired, the guard strengthened and the Welsh Bridge improved. However, Thomas Hunt drilled trained bands for Parliament under the town wall.

The situation in the town began to deteriorate as Ottley and Newport increased their efforts to recruit for the Royalist cause under the Commission of Array. When, in retaliation, William Pierpoint addressed a crowd to read Parliament's call to arms, a scuffle broke out in which Sir Paul Harris pulled off Pierpoint's cloak in an attempt to grab the Parliamentary declaration. Ottley then fought his way to the front brandishing a staff and heralded by a drummer. The meeting was closed when the Mayor Richard Gibbons threatened those who would not disperse with a charge of rioting. Both sides began drilling and parading openly. On August 2nd Sir Vincent Corbett marched eighty men across Atcham Bridge while Richard Lloyd did the same with a hundred at Montford Bridge. In town, Ottley inspected a force of over a hundred Royalist citizens. Brawls broke out in the evening between the two sides but no deaths occurred.

In September the House of Lords sent for the Parliamentarians Richard Owen and Richard Betton as delinquents. Betton fled, Owen was arrested, but a crowd of two hundred in Shrewsbury used force to release him. The Royalists eventually held sway, finally persuading the council on the 15th September to invite the King to the town. The King had given Ottley a commission to raise two hundred men to garrison Shrewsbury and he promptly moved these troops into the town to secure it. On the 19th September Charles stayed at Wellington and arrived in Shrewsbury the following day. After a brief visit to Chester to raise troops and money, he returned to Shrewsbury where he addressed the loyal gentry at Gay Meadow. In October he marched to Bridgnorth, en route to

Sir Vincent Corbet

B.1617 d.1656. The Corbets were an ancient and wealthy Shropshire family. Vincent Corbet was educated at Oxford and entered the legal profession in 1638. In 1640 he was returned to the House of Parliament as an MP for Shropshire. Corbet declared his support for the King before hostilities had broken out, was knighted in June 1641 and seven months later created a baronet. By 1642 he was a member of the Royalist Commission of Array and was drilling trained bands of men in the town of Shrewsbury, eventually receiving command of a regiment of horse and foot raised by the gentry and clergy of Shropshire.

It remains unclear as to the competence of Corbet as a military commander. On the one hand there is anecdotal evidence which suggests that he was inept. Brereton remarked that after an unsuccessful attempt to take Nantwich from the Parliamentary forces, Corbet was reduced to crawling away on all-fours lest he should be recognised and then running away bareheaded. Corbet claimed that he was "poorly served with raw soldiers and young commanders." In 1643 Vincent Corbet tried to hold Market Drayton with three hundred men, but before he could erect earthworks as a defensive fortification he was driven away from the town having been surprised in a dawn raid. Malbon relates that Corbet had to escape in "shirte and wascote". However, Corbet certainly saw a good deal of action in Shropshire and elsewhere. He led the Shrewsbury foot at Naseby and was involved in resisting several sieges, notably at High Ercall, Bridgnorth and the family seat at Moreton Corbet. Moreton Corbet Castle had been garrisoned for Charles I but was lost to Parliament in September 1644. The castle was destroyed and Vincent Corbet was fined £2,822.

London (on a course that was to lead him to clash with Parliament at Edgehill). At Bridgnorth he issued a proclamation accusing Thomas Hunt, Thomas Nicholls and Humphrey Mackworth of sedition. The pressure upon local people to oppose Parliament increased.

The prominent opponents now left Shrewsbury, while they still could, in the hope of organising elsewhere. Others remained, attempting to get on with their business as best they could, keeping their preferences secret. But as a list of 'delinquents' shows, this was not easy to do. Those listed in 1642 included:

William Rowley	*Beare brewer*
Owen George	
John Prowde	*Draper*
John Loyde	*Draper*
John Jeffreys	*Draper, Collector of the subsidie*
John Atcherley	
Adam Webb	
John Lowe	*Draper*
Thomas Clarke	*Butcher*
William Buttrey	*Trumpeter*
Richard Cheshire	
John Hopton	*That did carry the mace before the Commissioners of the Parliament*
John Mackworth	*Dier*

Those supporters of Parliament who stayed could expect to be constantly under threat. The author of an anonymous letter made accusations against Richard Proude "for he is the basest knave in towne and a traitor or hippocrite and Roundhead".

In Ludlow the people called for a peaceful resolution, primarily in the hope of preventing the dissolution of the Council of the Marches, for which most inhabitants blamed Parliament. Such was the economic and political significance to the town of the council that when war seemed unavoidable the majority supported the King.

Bridgnorth generally organised for the King and had mustered a local militia in August 1642 under Thomas Corbett of Longnor. The towns of Wem and Whitchurch also gave their initial support to Charles. On the other hand, the town of Oswestry was influenced by the support given to Parliament by a number of prominent local families such as the Lloyds of Aston, the Powells of Park, the Bakers of Sweeney, the Middletons of Chirk and the Myttons of Halston.

In general then, Shropshire was Royalist, the nobles and gentry having secured the initiative by early organisation and recruitment. Their influence on those beneath them in the social scale was immense. Walter Pigott of Chetwynd, who had been Sheriff of

King Charles 1 addressing the loyal Shropshire gentry at Gay Meadow, Shrewsbury, in 1642

Shropshire in 1624, was too old to fight for the King, but used his status to persuade or intimidate others to enlist. In January 1643 he had Andrew Mills of Newport sent to the Spring Assizes for trial on account of this gentleman "soliciting one Thomas Higgins, a soldier of Captain Robert Corbett, to leave his service and join Sir William Brereton" (a Parliamentarian).

Those who had strong religious feelings could not be intimidated by their 'superiors' and followed their conscience. However, many ordinary villagers and farmers who were tenants or whose livelihood depended on those above them would simply follow the lead of their employers. Richard Gough writes that the only man from Myddle to join the Parliamentary forces was John Mould. The Mould family of Myddle had worked for the Bakers of Sweeney. Such loyalty reflected the pragmatic necessity to keep on good terms with one's boss and, more significantly, the leadership by deference that such gentry wielded in local matters by nature of their education and rank. Several tenants on the estates of the Thynne family of Caus were pressured to fight for the King.

Some may have been swayed by the offer of cash for service. At Myddle Richard Gough recalled:

"I saw a multitude of men, and upon the highest banke of the hill I saw this Robert More standing, with a paper in his hand, and three or foure soldier's pikes, stick'd upright in the ground by him; and there hee made a proclamation, that if any person would serve the King, as a soldier in the wars, hee should have 14 groats a weeke for his pay."

Excitement and glory may have played a part in some men's decision to join up. The offer of adventure in a relatively static society must have appealed to some, particularly the young. In Defoe's 'Memoirs of a Cavalier' Andrew Newport, son of the prominent Royalist Richard Newport, confessed, "When I went into arms at the beginning of this war, I did not trouble myself to examine sides: I was glad to hear the drums beat for soldiers."

Some cases do exist of the war dividing whole families with brothers or fathers and sons fighting one another. William Littleton of Ludlow was a supporter of Parliament whilst his brothers were staunch Royalists. Avery Price from Holdgate Fee fought for Parliament whereas his brother Robert fought for the king. Thomas Edwards of Church Stretton was particularly active in raising troops and funds for the Royalist cause, while his elder brother Humphrey was a Parliamentarian who sat on the Commission which tried the King and signed his death warrant. The Earl of Denbigh was a Royalist and was killed at Cannock in April 1643; his son and heir supported Parliament, which added considerable weight to Parliament's cause in Shropshire and the West Midlands.

Though such cases are unusual they point to the dangers of assuming that certain specific groups all took one side or another. However, in the main those who were Catholic or High Church supported the king and those who were Puritan sided with Parliament. Those in the middle - people who had no strong leaning either way - were swayed by other considerations such as landlord pressure or short term gain. Geography was also a significant factor. In the more remote areas of the county, such as the south-west, people tried to stay out of the war as best they could. It was here that the Clubman movement (those who fought neither for the King nor Parliament, but to protect themselves against both) rose up in the later war years.

In the main Shropshire was under Royalist control at the start of the war with pockets of Parliament support largely confined to the northern regions and the south-western corner around Hopton Castle.

Chirk ❖

Whitchurch ★

Ellesmere ●

Market Drayton ★

● Oswestry

★ Wem

❖ Myddle

Moreton Corbet ●

Newport ✪

Shrawardine ●

Albright Hussey ●

High Ercall ●

Longford ★

River Severn

Lilleshall ●

Rowton Castle ●

Longner Hall ●

SHREWSBURY

Apley Castle ●

Caus Castle ●

Dawley ●

Wellington ✪

Shifnal ✪

Leigh Hall ●

Madeley ●

Tong ✪

Benthall ●

Montgomery ❖

Much Wenlock ●

Bridgnorth ●

Lea Hall ●

Church Stretton ●

Holgate Castle ●

Bishop's Castle ●

Broncroft Castle ●

Hopton Castle ★

Stokesay Castle ●

River Severn

● LUDLOW

Brampton Bryan Castle ★

0	miles 10
0	kms 10

● Royalist Control

★ Parliamentary Control

✪ Interchangeable Control

Location of main population centres and main garrisons - 1643
(also showing location of Myddle)

Chirk ❖

Ellesmere ★

★ Oswestry

★ Whitchurch

Market
Drayton ✪

★ Wem

❖ Myddle

Moreton
Corbet
★

Newport ✪

Shrawardine

● Longford
Lilleshall

River
Severn

● Albright Hussey

High Ercall
●

Rowton Castle
●

Longner Hall ●

SHREWSBURY

● Caus Castle

● Apley Castle

Dawley
●

✪ Wellington

● Shifnal
Tong

● Leigh Hall

● Madeley

Benthall
●

Montgomery ❖

Much
Wenlock
●

● Bridgnorth

Church
Stretton
●

● Lea Hall

Holgate
Castle
●

● Bishop's
Castle

● Broncroft Castle

River
Severn

Hopton
Castle
●

Stokesay
Castle
●

● LUDLOW

Brampton
Bryan
Castle
●

0   miles   10

0   kms   10

● Royalist Control

★ Parliamentary Control

✪ Interchangeable Control

Location of main population centres and main garrisons - 1644
(also showing location of Myddle)

Chirk ❖

Ellesmere ★

★ Oswestry

★ Whitchurch

Market
Drayton ✪

★ Wem

❖ Myddle

Moreton
Corbet ⚔

Newport ✪

Shrawardine ⚔

River
Severn

★ Albright Hussey

High Ercall ●

Longford
Lilleshall ★

● Longner Hall

● Apley Castle

Rowton Castle ⚔

SHREWSBURY

Dawley ✪ ● Wellington

Shifnal ✪

⚔ Caus Castle

● Leigh Hall

★ Madeley

Tong

Benthall ✪

Much
Wenlock ●

Bridgnorth ●

Montgomery ❖

⚔ Lea Hall

Church
Stretton ★

Holgate
Castle ⚔

✪ Bishop's
Castle

✪ Broncroft Castle

Hopton
Castle ⚔

Stokesay
Castle ★

● LUDLOW

Brampton
Bryan
Castle ⚔

0   miles   10

0   kms   10

● Royalist Control
★ Parliamentary Control
✪ Interchangeable Control
⚔ Dismantled by Royalists
⚔ Dismantled by Parliament

Location of main population centres and main garrisons - 1645
(also showing location of Myddle)

Great Shott and Granadoes

The Conduct of the War in Shropshire

Early Engagements

By the end of 1642 the King had appointed Sir Nicholas Byron as Colonel General of Cheshire and Shropshire, while Parliament requested John Corbett to raise troops in Shropshire. In December, eighty Royalist gentry agreed to raise a regiment of dragoons under Sir Vincent Corbet.

In Shropshire the war was fought through a series of sieges and skirmishes as each side attempted to win control of areas piece by piece. Castles and fortified manor houses were of prime importance as they could house garrisons to control the local area that in turn provided supplies and money through taxation. There were no large open battles in the county, but that is not to say that Shropshire was not affected by larger battles elsewhere. Troops leaving to fight at Edgehill and Marston Moor obviously left garrisons undermanned which could lead to their fall.

Little fighting in Shropshire took place until May 1643 when Whitchurch was taken by Parliamentary troops under the command of Sir William Brereton moving south from his Cheshire base. A hundred and fifty Royalists were killed. In the same month Shrewsbury was occupied by Royalist troops under Lord Capel and Oswestry garrisoned in July. In September Parliament forces entered Market Drayton and went on to fortify Wem under Sir Thomas Mytton and Sir William Brereton.

Lord Capel wasted little time in amassing four thousand men on Prees Heath to retake the town for the King. He attacked an outpost at Loppington but was repulsed by soldiers from the Wem garrison. On the 17th October 1643 Capel, with reinforcements, attacked the town itself. The battle raged for two days until the outnumbered Parliamentarians inflicted a bloody defeat on the Royalists. "Six carriages of bodies were taken away and thirty left on the ground".

Lord Capel

The Lord Capel, with a thousand and a Half
Came to Barton's Crosse and there they killed a Calfe
And stayinge there until the breake of Daye
They tooke their heeles and fast they fled away
(Parliamentary verse)

B.1610 d.1649. Arthur, Lord Capel was MP for Hertfordshire. Although he presented grievances against the King to the Long Parliament on behalf of his constituents, complaining against Ship Money and other measures, he was not prepared to support military action against the monarchy and sided with Charles during the Civil War. He was sent to Shrewsbury in 1643 to become Lieutenant General of Shropshire, Cheshire and North Wales. At the end of the war he accompanied the Queen to France and stayed in Jersey. Soon after, he returned to his own house at Hadham having had his estates sequestrated.

Capel helped the King to escape to the Isle of Wight and Parliament held him largely responsible for the renewal of the Civil War in 1648. He was impeached for high treason by Parliament for which he was beheaded in 1649. However, this was not before Capel made a daring escape from the Tower by lowering himself out of a window with some rope. After spending three days hiding in the Temple he was betrayed by a Thames boatman who had carried him to Lambeth Marsh.

Capel apparently met his fate with dignity. He addressed the onlookers, saying, "Pray at the moment of striking, join your Prayers; but make no noise (turning to his servants) it is inconvenient at this time".

The inscription on his tomb reads:

"Hereunder lieth interred the body of Arthur, Lord Capel, Baron of Hadham, who was murdered for his loyalty to King Charles the First, March 9th 1649".

Capel was largely ineffective as a military leader and struggled to maintain support for the King in Shrewsbury. He suffered a humiliating defeat at Wem in 1643. A letter from a soldier to his family blamed the army's lack of courage which, it claimed:

"moved my Lord's stomach so much, that after shedding tears of rage and anger he would not remove out of those trenches which he had so lately mastered, although they made many desperate shots at him, until he had taken out his pipe, and his friends in a manner forced him away."

This, however, is at odds with other accounts, which suggest that during the battle, His Lordship had simply sat some distance away smoking his pipe.

Brereton and his army were absent from the town, ironically in pursuit of Capel who they believed to be in the vicinity of Nantwich. Samuel Garbett noted that this left "only forty soldiers and an undisciplined rabble of men and women." The efforts of this small force according to Richard Baxter "did much daunt the enemy, seeing by all to be as of one mind resolved to fight and stand it out to the last man." It is difficult to see how Capel could have lost with an army that greatly outnumbered the opposition and which was better equipped. At the start of the war both sides relied on leaders who had little or no experience, holding their command because of their social status. On the Parliamentary side Sir William Brereton, however, appears to have been a very efficient leader both as a tactician and organiser. Being well led at this stage was often a matter of luck.

Sir William Brereton

B.1604 d.1661. William Brereton was the son of William Brereton of Handforth, Cheshire. He represented his home county as an MP in 1627-1628 and 1639-40, and was known for his Puritan sympathies. On the outbreak of hostilities he was appointed Commander-in-Chief of Parliamentary forces in Cheshire and the neighbouring counties to the south. He greatly affected the course of the war in Shropshire, especially in the north of the county, and provided much military support for the activities of the Parliamentary Committee of Shropshire based at Wem. Despite having no previous military experience, Brereton is generally viewed as a competent leader. Clarendon noted that he executed his "commands with notable Sobriety and indefatigable Industry".

Brereton is of interest to the historian because of the survival of his letter books dated 1645-1646. These give an extremely detailed picture of the war. In particular, they demonstrate the difficulties that communications posed for commanding officers and how important it was to ascertain the whereabouts of the opposition through the establishment of an efficient intelligence network.

The War Intensifies

On the 28th December Tong Castle also fell to Parliament, this time to forces from Eccleshall. In January 1644, Mytton surprised Royalists near Ellesmere, capturing both arms and prisoners, including Sir Nicholas Byron and Sir Richard Willis. The King quickly realised that a strong leader was required in the West and appointed Prince Rupert as Captain General of Royalist forces in Worcestershire, Shropshire and North Wales.

In February 1644 the experienced Prince Rupert arrived in Shropshire finding the Royalist finances and military organisation in a state of collapse. One senior commander had referred to Ottley, the Governor of Shrewsbury, as a "doting old fool". The town of Shrewsbury was disaffected, as were the inhabitants of Ludlow who compiled numerous complaints concerning taxation, billeting and soldiers' discipline. Rupert set about restoring the situation, imposing a county levy of 6d. in the pound on all men's estates, and sent in strong commanders such as Sir Michael Woodhouse, who immediately signalled his intentions by hanging a guard for sleeping on duty.

Meanwhile the glorious amateur Thomas Mytton, a resourceful and adventurous leader, planned to capture Oswestry by luring the Royalist Governor, Colonel Edward Lloyd, away from his command. The plan was to provide an invitation to a bogus dinner engagement some distance away. Mytton hoped to capture him on arrival and then force the surrender of the town. The plan failed when two of Mytton's scouts were captured and forced to reveal the ruse, causing Lloyd to return to Oswestry. While this plan may seem far-fetched, it apparently worked some days later on Sir Thomas Eyton at Buildwas.

Such eccentric actions were to be the exception, however, and the siege of Hopton Castle signalled a hardening of attitudes that became more common as the war progressed. In February 1644, thirty-one Parliamentary soldiers held out against a Royalist force of about five hundred horse and foot for two weeks. In such strongholds relatively few numbers could keep out a much larger army for many days and inflict heavy casualties. As Colonel Samuel More, commander of the garrison, recalled, "They shot 96 shot at our outer wall, and made a breach, which we defended for the space of two hours at least. So we gave them repulse with the loss of one man that was killed with a common shot, and three or four that were hurt, but they lost, as they said after wards, 150 of theirs."

Eventually the Royalists mined underneath the castle and More agreed to surrender in the belief that he and his soldiers should march away with their lives. Mercurius Britanicus (a Parliamentarian pamphleteer) reported that:

"Mr More was seized upon, and carried away prisoner, and the 24 souldiers tied back to back, and then some of them had their hands cut off; some with a hand, parte of an arme, and the rest cut and mangled both on hands and armes, and then all of them throwne into a muddy pit, where as often as any of them endeavoured to raise themselves out of the mud, striving to prolong

their miserable lives, they were straight by these bloody villains beate down into the mud again with great stones, which they hurled at them, and in this sad manner lamentably perished. Two maids were in the Castle, one they killed, and the other they wounded, and let her go, bidding her to go to Brampton Castle and tell her brother roundheads there, so they would serve them next."

It is doubtful that the war was ever a gentlemanly conflict, a myth created by several Victorian historians and artists and perpetuated by subsequent generations. However, acts of chivalry did sometimes occur, though often these had a pragmatic origin. In particular, the practice of allowing garrisons to march away or of prisoner exchange seems generous in the context of modern warfare. Armies had enough problems feeding themselves without the added strain of prisoners and had few secure places to keep them. Furthermore, in this kind of seesaw war one could be victor one week and vanquished the next, and so a little mercy could go a long way.

Any romance the war had held was by now wearing thin, as the number of soldiers who were killed or wounded increased rapidly. The bulk of the forces were drawn from the ranks of the ordinary working population. Many travelled far from their homes and some never returned. Robert Oldroyd, for example, was a clothworker from Heckmondwike, West Riding, one of many Yorkshire Parliamentarians who saw service in Shropshire. Oldroyd died in March 1644 from wounds sustained in an attack upon Market Drayton by Prince Rupert and his men.

Casualties

At Myddle, Gough refers to twenty men from the parish going to fight, of whom thirteen were killed. He lists how each died:

"First, Thomas Formeston, of Marton, a very hopefull young man, but at what place hee was killed I cannot say. Secondly ... Nat. Owen was mortally wounded by some of his owne party, in an alehouse quarrell, neare Bridgnorth, and was carryed in a cart to Bridgenorth to bee healed, but in the meane time the parliament party laid seidge to Bridgenorth, and the garrison soldiers within the towne sett the towne on fire, and fled into the castle, in which fire, this Owen (being unable to helpe himselfe) was burnt to death."

Others included Richard Chaloner "beeing a bigge lad, went to Shrewsbury, and was there listed, and went to Edghill fight ... and was never heard afterwards in this country", Reece Vaughan and John Arthurs "killed at Hopton Castle in this county", Thomas Taylor "killed I think at Oswestry" while "William Preece of the cave (who was commonly called Scogan of the Goblin hole) went for a soldier in the king's service and three of his sons (i.e.) Francis, Edward, and William, two of them viz. Francis and William were killed at High Ercall. The old man died in his bed, and Edward was hanged for stealing horses".

The number of Myddle parishioners killed represents a high mortality rate (i.e. 65% of those who enlisted), but one should remember the conditions that soldiers fought and lived under. Weapons of the period created savage and deep wounds. The pike, an extremely long spear of twelve to eighteen feet topped with metal was the common weapon of the foot soldier. Other foot soldiers, the musketeers, carried the cumbersome matchlock, difficult to load and prone to accident. In addition, the infantry would carry swords, as did the cavalry who would also be armed with pistols or carbines. Artillery was not only used in siege situations, but also in open battles to devastating effect. When dirt entered a wound the chances of healing was further reduced. The medical facilities and treatment of wounds were extremely basic, while blood poisoning and secondary infection often followed. Surgery was primitive and usually meant amputation, no blood transfusion existed and many wounds proved to be fatal. Furthermore, good surgeons were in short supply. In 1643 Sir Vincent Corbet wrote to Francis Ottley in Shrewsbury:

> "Some of our men are dayly hurt, and cannot avoid much prejudice without a Surgeon to apply remedyes. In regard whereof I pray you do me the favour to send young Shelvocke, or some other good Surgeon whom you will recommend me, with all speed to Malpas, where I and my regiment are now quartered; and let him bring with him his Implements, & all manner of necessaries."

Disease carried by the troops living in unsanitary conditions was also rife. Plague and typhus (army fever) affected soldiers and the civilian populations they encountered. Parish records note many deaths of soldiers that were not necessarily the result of combat. The Churchwardens' accounts for Ludlow in 1643 solemnly note: "Paid for Shrouds for the Buryall of seven souldiers here ... 16s. 6d."

The scale of fighting in the war has often been underestimated. Whilst there were few major open battles in Shropshire, so called skirmishes could result in high casualty rates, as could frontal attacks on fortified positions. The burial registers of many Shropshire parishes highlight some of those who were killed. It is not suprising to find numerous entries in the local burial register after the fighting at Whitchurch in May 1643. Many died slowly of their wounds. They included:

May 30.	The Kannaneer with 17 soldiers moore slene
May 31.	Frances Boland buried with the aforsayd slene men
June 6.	A prisoner
June 20.	6 soldiers buried
June 21.	2 prisoners

Being a prisoner could obviously be fatal. Captain Wingate, a prisoner of the Royalists in Ludlow, claimed: "Some other Prisoners ... they have also put in a close Prison, using them in the extremist cruelty that may be devised, allowing them only bread and water for their sustestation, and so little, that if they long continue there, they will be starved to death."

During the years of fighting, the register of Whitchurch also records many deaths, including in September 1644, "a soldier that was stabbed". Significant research has estimated that the mortality rate in the Civil War was probably equal in effect to that of the First World War in terms of relative population. It is hardly suprising that some soldiers deserted. John Van Byrusch reported to Prince Rupert that conditions in Much Wenlock caused "many of my soldiers out of a discontented minde too runn away".

As the war of attrition progressed through February and March 1644, Albright Hussey and Moreton Corbet Castle were fortified for the King and Brampton Bryan sieged. Rupert took Market Drayton killing twenty-two Parliamentarians and capturing forty, whilst Apley Castle was lost and retaken by Vaughan who destroyed it. At Longford, in April 1644, when the Parliamentary garrison surrendered to Royalist forces, one hundred musketeers were allowed to march away without arms. Tong Castle was also re-taken from Parliament.

Prince Rupert of the Rhine (1619-1682), the King's nephew and commander of Royalist forces in and around Shropshire

Prince Rupert

B.1619 d.1682. He was the son of Frederick of the Palatinate and Elizabeth the daughter of James I. Born in Prague he spent most of his youth in Holland after his parents had been ousted from their territories during the Thirty Years War. As a teenager, he was involved in various continental campaigns and was therefore an experienced soldier by the time he arrived in England to assist his uncle, Charles I, in 1642. Rupert was renowned as being a flamboyant cavalry commander and his reputation as an outstanding leader grew throughout the war to the point where all kinds of fabulous powers and deeds were ascribed to him. His pet poodle "Boy" was supposed to be a witch that could speak in Hebrew and could catch musket balls in its mouth.

Rupert's military experience also made him an able administrator who spent a good deal of time in Shropshire during the war, even though there were no major battles in the county. He effectively organised the Royalist war effort in the Marches.

Rupert is remembered in Shrewsbury by giving his name to the Prince Rupert Hotel, formerly Jones' Mansion, where he stayed. Rupert was eventually defeated in the field when the Parliamentary New Model Army began to emerge as a more disciplined and effective force than its Royalist opposition. After surrendering Bristol he was cashiered by Charles, and although subsequently vindicated by a court martial, he left England in 1646. He carried on the war effort in 1649-1652 as an admiral and returned to England during the Restoration.

The failed attempt by Lord Byron to take Wem for the King in April 1644 marked a change in the fortunes of Parliament. Although close to defeat with no provisions left, the defenders hung on and Byron not realising how close he was to victory gave up the siege. Had Wem fallen the Royalists would have controlled the county, but as it was, Wem's survival lifted Parliament's morale, and in the coming months they began to turn the tables around.

Irish troops and Mercenaries

Irish troops were used by Byron to attack Wem. Brought over to fight for the king, many of these were in fact Anglo-Irish, English soldiers who had seen service in Ireland. Parliament purposefully labelled them all as 'Irish'. This was blatant propaganda to arouse anti-Catholic prejudice. Captain Sir William Vaughan raised a regiment of Anglo-Irish and brought them to England in 1643. By 1644 they had, according to the diary of Richard Symonds, made garrisons in Shrawardine Castle, Caus Castle, High Ercall, Lilleshall and Dawley. A detachment served in Ludlow, while there are examples of others fighting on the Shropshire-Cheshire border. It was not uncommon for these men to change sides. Sir William Brereton's letters show captured soldiers put into Parliament's service along the Welsh border. Writing to her husband Luke, Mrs Lloyd remarked: "This week there are garrisons put in Feneshall and Bettisfield. We expect more to Hanmer. They are of those men that came from Ireland that turned when they were taken prisoners."

When Parliament surrendered Apley Castle, Irish troops were in the garrison. They were allowed either to march away to the garrison at Wem or to take service with Sir William Vaughan's regiment. This meant changing sides for a second time.

The Irish were not the only foreign troops in Shropshire. In addition to dignitaries such as Prince Rupert and Prince Maurice, numerous mercenaries fought for the Royalists. They included the Dutchmen Major Boza, John Van Byrusch, Colonel Vangeris, and the Florentine John Davallier. Others fought for Parliament. In a letter to the Earl of Essex, Prince Rupert revealed, "I have taken prisoners of those who have taken up arms against His Majestie of all nations, English, Scottish, Irish, French, Dutch, Walloons, of all religions and opinions."

Often they were valued for their expertise, having seen service in the religious wars on the continent. Only a few Englishmen fighting in Shropshire such as William Preece of Myddle who "went for a soldier into the Low Countries" had experience of war. Mercenaries could also provide specific skills in explosives or engineering - vital in a war largely concerned with sieges. As time went by, however, the English troops gained such experience and mercenaries were valued less and often resented by the end of the war.

Parliament grows stronger

May 1644 saw Parliament capture a hundred Royalists at Montford Bridge and in June their luck had changed for the better when Denbigh and Mytton managed to capture Oswestry and, despite an attack by five thousand Royalists in July, held onto it.

Parliament was gradually improving its organisation within Shropshire. The Parliamentary Committee which sat at Wem was often divided and at odds with one another, with petty jealousies coming to the fore. Denbigh's installation of Mytton as Governor of Oswestry enraged other members of the Committee who had not been consulted. When they confronted Denbigh, he "told Mr Mackworth, one of the Committee, that he was a rascal and a liar, and that he would cudgel him; he said that all the Committee were knaves, and had cheated the country; he also threatened to run Mackworth through with his sword."

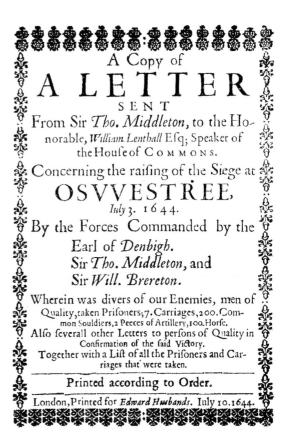

A Copy of
A LETTER
SENT
From Sir *Tho. Middleton*, to the Honorable, *William Lenthall* Esq; Speaker of the House of COMMONS.
Concerning the raising of the Siege at
OSVVESTREE.
Iuly 3. 1644.
By the Forces Commanded by the Earl of *Denbigh*.
Sir *Tho. Middleton*, and Sir *Will. Brereton.*
Wherein was divers of our Enemies, men of Quality, taken Prisoners; 7. Carriages, 200. Common Souldiers, 2 Peeces of Artillery, 100. Horse. Also severall other Letters to persons of Quality in Confirmation of the said Victory. Together with a List of all the Prisoners and Carriages that were taken.

Printed according to Order.

London, Printed for *Edward Husbands*. Iuly 10. 1644.

Tract recording Parliament's capture of Oswestry, 1644. The commander, Earl Denbigh, later fell foul of the Shropshire Committee

Finally in July 1644, some members of the Committee, together with Brereton, conspired to remove Denbigh by levelling serious accusations against him. Denbigh was summoned to London to answer the charges and eventually lost his commission. At the same time, the Committee secured the services of a mercenary, Colonel Reinking, to bring a more professional approach to the conduct of the war. He was later to clash bitterly with the flamboyant Mytton who, during August, continued to harry the Royalist forces around Shrewsbury. In the Welsh marches he captured three hundred and eighty men at Welshpool and in September Montgomery Castle was taken. Meanwhile Reinking proved his ability by taking Moreton Corbet Castle.

This action highlighted the difficulties of communication in the war. Messages were relayed by hand and the size and whereabouts of the enemy was often unclear. Commanders were therefore expected to act on their own initiative, and Reinking showed his experience and cunning by ordering drummers to be placed at some distance apart as the attack began, in order to give the impression of a much larger force. Reinking gave various noisy commands to imaginary regiments to reinforce this deceit and over eighty officers and men inside the garrison surrendered.

Parliament was tightening its grip across the north of the county and began to fix its eyes on the prize of Shrewsbury. In October, Mytton in his own inimitable fashion was unlucky not to take Shrawardine Castle. The Governor of the castle, Sir William Vaughan, was attending communion in the local church with twelve of his local officers when Mytton arrived and captured them. Mytton paraded his prisoners in front of the walls and pointed a gun to Vaughan's head and ordered him to tell the garrison to surrender. Remarkably, Vaughan managed to break free and cross the drawbridge, which was then closed behind him. Mytton had to be content with the twelve prisoners.

As the winter drew on, significant changes in command were confirmed. Parliament sacked Denbigh while

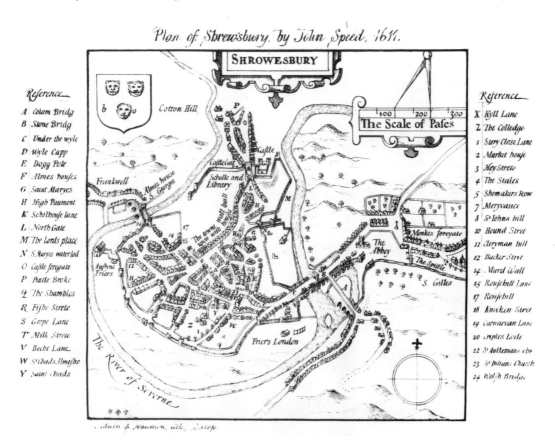

John Speed's map of Shrewsbury, 1610, showing details of the Town Wall and Castle

Shrewsbury Castle and Castlegates, one of the sites where Parliament breached the town's ancient walled defences in 1645

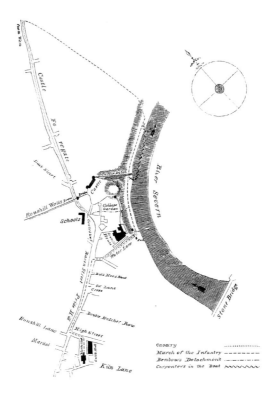

The movement of Parliamentary forces taking Shrewsbury in 1645, described by Owen & Blakeway, 1825

Colonel Thomas Mytton (1597?-1656) of Halston,
a resourceful Parliamentary commander

Thomas Mytton

"Colonel Mitton is a very gallant Soldier and one that is full of Valour and Cordial for the Publicke good as appears by all his Actions, he having in all that he hath done received but very little pay, yet is not any the less active in preferring the Publicke before his own interest..."

B.1597? d.1656 Son of Richard Mytton of Halston, Shropshire. He was appointed as one of the Committee for Shropshire by Parliament in 1643. Mytton's notable successes in Shropshire included the defence of Wem and the capture of Oswestry for which he was appointed Governor. He claimed responsibility for the taking of Shrewsbury though this was hotly disputed by the Dutchman Reinking. After Sir Thomas Middleton retired his commission under the self-denying ordinance of 1645, Mytton was made commander-in-chief of the six counties of North Wales and High Sheriff of Shropshire, and later vice-admiral of North Wales. He represented Shropshire in Cromwell's first Parliament.

Mytton was notable for his daring and cunning. This led some people to portray him in the role of the romantic, dashing hero. However, his unpredictable nature did not always endear him to his peers. He also indulged in self-promotion and sought to increase his power. A picture of Mytton's character emerges in his management of the election for a Knight of the Shire in 1646. The freeholders understood the election would be at Oswestry at nine a.m. but soon discovered that Mytton, in league with the Under-Sheriff, had moved the vote to ten in the village of Alberbury. Arriving at nine, Mytton read the writ and closed the voting before the outwitted electors arrived from Oswestry, thus ensuring the election of his candidate Humphrey Edwards.

He died in London and was buried in St. Chad's church in Shrewsbury in 1656.

the King appointed Prince Maurice as Major General of Worcestershire, Shropshire, Herefordshire and Monmouth allowing Rupert to be promoted to command the Royalist field army. He arrived in February 1645 and despite an attack on Frankwell on the 9th that resulted in several Royalist casualties, promptly gathered his forces together and marched into Wales to confront Brereton. Having taken the best of the garrison with him, the town's defences were woefully weak and the Parliamentarians realised that this was their best chance of taking the town. With twelve hundred men they approached during the early morning of February 22nd under the cover of darkness.

The fall of Shrewsbury

The successful attack hinged upon a group of eight carpenters, who in a boat, arrived on the town side of the palisade, underneath the castle, and began to saw it down. It seemed strange that the sentries did not detect this commotion, and most contemporary

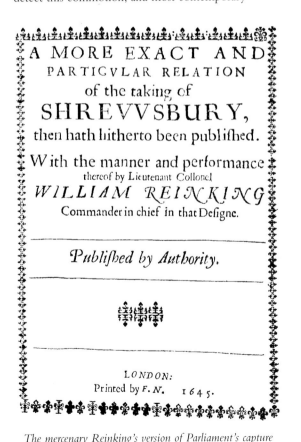

The mercenary Reinking's version of Parliament's capture of Shrewsbury, 1645

writers came to the conclusion that they must have been treacherous. By the time other soldiers of the garrison had realised what was happening it was too late. A breach had been made and the Parliamentary soldiers were able to gain entry into the preliminary defences. Captain Benbow, a native of the town, scaled the walls and headed for the north or castle gates. Whether Benbow opened the gates, enabling Reinking to enter the town with the main body of troops via Water Lane, or the gates were left open by someone who was sympathetic to Parliament is unclear. In particular, Sir William Owen, who lived in the Council House, came under suspicion.

Reinking and Mytton both claimed that they were responsible for the capture of Shrewsbury in 1645. Mytton was called to the House of Commons on 29th March and thanked for his efforts – particularly the capture of the town. Reinking disputed that Mytton deserved the credit and went to the trouble of writing to Parliament giving his account of events. His published letter entitled, "A more exact and particular relation of the taking of Shrewsbury than hath hitherto been published. With the manner and performance thereof by William Reinking commander in chief in that design", portrayed Mytton as only a minor player on the field of battle. While preparing to enter Shrewsbury Reinking reported: "About this time came in Colonel Mytton ... unexpected of me, and as one of the Committee, he fell in and kept himself with them."

In response, Mytton produced his own reply that showed himself in a more heroic role. It noted that "Colonel Mytton led on the horse", furthermore the good people of Shrewsbury were "no little glad that Colonel Mytton hath taken it, and accordingly expressed themselves to the Committee". It appears that both Mytton and Reinking hoped to be appointed Governor of Shrewsbury. Indeed, Mytton's account of events concluded: "The whole County ... desire that Colonel Mitton be made Governor thereof; who is an honest cordiall well affected man, and of true integrity." Eventually Sir Humphrey Mackworth was appointed governor in June 1645 thus thwarting both men's ambition.

The garrison was allowed to withdraw to Ludlow with the exception of thirteen Irish troops who were hanged by order of a Parliamentary ordinance reflecting the Puritan hatred of Catholicism and the increasing savagery of the war. In March, Rupert hanged thirteen prisoners at Whitchurch in reprisal and wrote to the Earl of Essex in justification, "I would not be doing my duty if I had not let those that massacred them know that their own must pay the price for their inhumanity."

In April, Parliament passed the Self-Denying Ordinance that excluded all Members of Parliament from serving in the New Model Army. In effect this enabled Parliament to encourage leadership by ability rather than simply social rank. Only a few exceptions such as Cromwell, Brereton and Sir Thomas Middleton were allowed to continue because of their obvious worth. As the organisation of the Parliamentarian war effort steadily improved, so the Royalist cause deteriorated. Parliament not only controlled London, Britain's major port and commercial centre, but also the wealthier and more prosperous farmland of the eastern counties. This gave them access to a more regular income.

Clubmen

The system set up by Parliament provided more money than the King could muster, having to rely on confiscation, forced loans, gifts and excise duty, unable as he was to levy regular taxes through Parliament. The longer the war continued the more pressured was the Royalist search for finance. At a local level this resulted in ad hoc taxation or duties imposed by local commanders, and more importantly increased looting which enraged the civilian population, further damaging the Royalist cause. This lead directly to the Clubmen movement in the south-west, which emerged gradually during the winter of 1644-5 as Parliament increased their hold on the north of the county.

The so-called 'Marcher Associations' formed in 1644, were an attempt to secure the loyalty of the civilian populations in Royalist held areas to prevent the spread of Parliamentarian control. In March 1644 the Royalist gentry of the area around Ludlow met and called up a local defence force the Posse Comitatus. This was an ancient power whereby the Sheriff was enabled to recruit all able-bodied men in a situation of emergency. The Association that the gentry proposed would be on a much larger scale. Linking Shropshire, Worcestershire, and later Herefordshire and Staffordshire, it would arm the local population. This, of course, was in itself a dangerous step as once armed, they could turn just as easily against

the Royalists themselves. To avert this the King agreed to the plan with the proviso that Royalist army officers under the overall control of Prince Maurice would command them. However, the plan was greeted with horror by the Royalist officers who garrisoned the area because it was to be financed through the proceeds of local sequestration and taxes that they themselves already depended on. The proposed plans certainly focused the minds of the local people, together with the increased pressure upon the local garrison commanders to obtain adequate supplies, an explosive situation arose.

The Parliamentary Mercurius Britannicus claimed that "A thousand in armes", rose up to demand the removal of the Royalist commander, a Dutchman called Vangeris. Their claim for compensation was seemingly sparked off by the excessive behaviour of his troops. The writer stated:

> "Neither for the King nor for the Parliament, but stand only upon their own guard for the preservation of their lives and fortunes ...
> They are absolutely resolved ... not to lay down their armes unless his Majesty grant them their own conditions which are these:
>
> (1) to have restitution of all wrongs done by Van Gore.
> (2) to have him and all his soldiers expelled their Country.
> (3) that the King's two garrisons at Hopesay House, and Lea House shall be removed and demolished.
> (4) that they may have commanders of their own."

This piece of Parliamentarian propaganda is misleading in that it gives the impression of an armed rising against the King. Certainly meetings took place. In a letter dated 3rd January 1645 Sir Michael Earnley referred to some "seditious people in the county who have mustered three thousand" and a letter from Sir Michael Woodhouse on the 22nd February 1645 mentions a recent rebellion in the area, although these could be exaggerated. Some leaders or representatives must have existed, however, to draft the demands of the meetings and seem to have been mostly clergy and minor gentry. Gervase Needham the vicar of Bishop's Castle, initially voicing some support for the King, was considered to be a "moderate Puritan". Richard Heath who was curate of Clunbury and Francis Harris of

Aston were both opponents of Laudian reform as was Jeremiah Powell, nephew of Erasmus Powell a Puritan and late parson of Clun, and the cousin of Vavasour Powell a "Fifth Monarchist".

It is quite possible that some of the Clubmen leaders may have seen this situation as an opportunity to turn the discontent into a pro-Parliamentarian movement. In effect a hearts and minds campaign for the loyalty of the civilian population was being conducted. However, there is no evidence that fighting took place between Clubmen and the Royalist troops at this stage. Despite their demands, the only one to be met was the removal of Vangeris from the area. They did not attack the local garrisons and their request for their own commanders hints towards a desire for independence. The lesser gentry who led the Clubmen may have had more Parliamentarian leanings, but one of the leaders, Needham, had suffered earlier at the hands of Parliament when his house was burnt and he was forbidden to run a small school as his livelihood – unlikely credentials for a fervent Parliamentarian. The overriding concern of the rank and file seems to have been to stay neutral or they would have taken further action once their demands were not met.

The campaign for local allegiance continued as the war dragged towards its end. By the summer of 1645, the situation had changed in the south-west of the county and the Royalist hold was fading. The church at Bishop's Castle was used to quarter eighty horse and eighty foot under the command of Major Fenwick for Parliament. On August 25th a Royalist raiding party comprised of troops from Bridgnorth and Ludlow set out to attack the local fair in order to plunder supplies. They were not successful on this occasion. In a letter to William Lenthall the Parliamentary Committee rejoiced:

"It hath pleased God to give us a further evidence of his goodness by delivering into our hands 140 of the enemies forces belonging unto Ludlow, who amongst others to the number of 300 were sent under the command of Colonel Davelier towards Bishop's Castle to plunder the country ... After some hurt done, our forces consisting of 80 horse and 80 foot, under the command of Major Fenwick, which quartered

Sir William Vaughan

D. 1649. Vaughan was governor of Shrawardine Castle. It was from this association that his nickname "the Devil of Shrawardine" is derived. Little is known of his early career, but at the beginning of 1644 he was sent from Dublin with a hundred and sixty Horse to Cheshire, joining with Lord Byron's army. From his stronghold at Shrawardine, he constantly harassed Parliament. In March 1644, he took Apley Castle and defeated Thomas Mytton near Longford.

Despite a narrow escape from capture in October 1644, Vaughan's position was further improved when he was made General of Shropshire, and it allowed him to prosecute the war in a more ruthless manner, which brought about his nickname. Of his activities around Chirk, a Puritan woman is supposed to have prayed " O' Lord ... O curse with a heavy curse the Great Devil of Shrawardine, what doth torment thy children".

However, Shrawardine was left in the hands of his brother Dr James Vaughan, a parson. James did not have his brother's military skill and Shrawardine duly capitulated to Parliament.

In 1645 Vaughan accompanied the King from Shropshire to Naseby. Following Charles' defeat, he headed back to Shropshire where at times he appeared to provide the only effective opposition to the local Parliamentary forces, which included the relief of High Ercall and campaigns in the south-west of the county and the Welsh Borders. On the 1st November 1645, his army was severely beaten at Denbigh by a Parliamentary army led by his old adversary, Colonel Thomas Mytton. Later he was routed by Brereton at Stow-on-the-Wold in Gloucestershire.

At the end of the first Civil War he appears to have fled to The Hague and then to have fought in Ireland. Vaughan was killed on the 2nd August 1649 at Rathmines apparently dying "bravely at the head of his men".

in Bishop's Castle for securing that town and parts adjacent, drew forth, and within a mile of that place, with the assistance of some countrymen that were got into a body, charged the enemy. Our forlorn foot soldiers retreated disorderly, but our horse did second them so gallantly that, after a hot charge, they wholly routed the enemy, brought off all the prisoners to the number above specified, whereof almost 20 were Commission Officers: and we are credibly informed that there came not above 40 back to Ludlow, besides those which were brought wounded in carts."

Here we have direct evidence of countrymen actually taking arms and involving themselves in the fighting. They abandoned their neutrality when their region was mostly under Parliamentary control to assist their forces against the Royalists.

In retribution for this assistance, Sir William Vaughan attacked the town and as an act of reprisal damaged the church, as it had been used by the Parliamentary troops and for "the preaching of sedition". Part of the town was also burnt. Though Vaughan left some troops to control the area these were driven out by Sir Thomas Middleton and the garrison at Lea Castle finally departed.

Vaughan's troops, however, were still harassing the district in October 1645 when marching for Chester. Contemporary sources noted that "they lay at Bishop's Castle ... the foot sore weary with the long march from Weobley". Again, Parliament was equal to the task as "Col. Hungerford, Governor of Stokesay, sent a party of 6 firelocks to alarm them at Bishop's Castle". Vaughan was finally defeated later that month in Denbighshire.

Royalist desperation

In the north of the county, 1645 saw increased fighting, as the Royalist cause grew more desperate. In April, Parliament suffered five hundred killed and wounded in an attempt to take the fortified manor house of High Ercall. In May the King passed through Newport and Market Drayton in an attempt to relieve Chester. Meanwhile, several more Royalist garrisons fell to Parliament at Leigh Hall near Worthen, Longner, Atcham, Tong, Rowton Castle and Madeley.

Madeley had been important because of its iron works and position on the river. Furnaces and forges in Shropshire supplied armies in other parts of the country. Writing to Sir Richard Lloyd, the Royalist Orlando Bridgeman noted, "I understand this Mathias Gervise hath at Layton (Leighton forge) beyond Shrewsbury one tunne of battery shott and a Tonne of Granadoes ... what must bee done with it I know not, it is not safe letting them stay where they are, and I wish the granadoes ... were sent forthwith to Oxford."

In an era when road transport was virtually non-existent, the River Severn was essential, particularly as a trading route to the port of Bristol. In Shropshire the Severn was the main artery of trade and communication. During the Civil War it carried soldiers, arms, food and fuel. The Parliamentary Committee for Shropshire, highlighting the importance of local mineral deposits and their proximity to the river, wrote to Brereton in April 1645 stating:

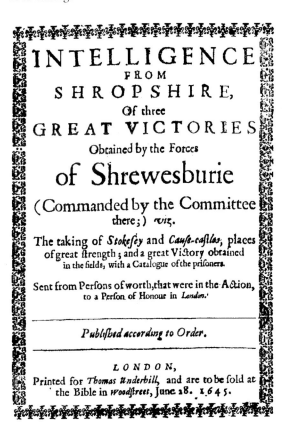

INTELLIGENCE
FROM
SHROPSHIRE,
Of three
GREAT VICTORIES
Obtained by the Forces
of Shrewesburie
(Commanded by the Committee
there;) *viz.*

The taking of *Stokesey* and *Cause-caslles*, places of great strength; and a great Victory obtained in the fields; with a Catalogue of the prisoners.

Sent from Persons of worth, that were in the Action, to a Person of Honour in *London.*

Published according to Order.

LONDON,
Printed for *Thomas Underhill*, and are to be sold at the Bible in *Woodstreet*, June 28. 1645.

Parliamentary tract celebrating victories in Shropshire in 1645

*High Ercall House: Seat of the Newport Family and a Royalist garrison.
It was the scene of two hard sieges towards the end of the war*

"We lately erected a small garrison at Benthall near those places whence we have all our coal and lime for this garrison, the same, being within a mile from the river, is of much concernment to us because of carriage by water."

With the decisive defeat of the King's field army at Naseby in June, the Parliamentary forces renewed their onslaught on the Royalist garrisons. Reinking led five hundred foot and three hundred horse towards Ludlow, capturing Stokesay and Broncroft Castles without a fight. A Royalist attempt to retake Stokesay ended in a bloody engagement at Wistanstow where they lost a hundred dead and three hundred prisoners. Further west, Caus Castle was taken along with Shrawardine. In July, Parliament destroyed the latter as well as Rowton. However, High Ercall still remained a thorn in Parliament's side and a further attempt to take it ended in Reinking's capture and a hundred dead.

As Charles became increasingly desperate he returned to Shropshire, and moving via Ludlow and Bridgnorth, attempted to link up with Royalist forces in Cheshire. Such was the tightening Parliamentary grip on the local garrisons that Brereton and Middleton were able to foil this attempt and Charles retreated.

By August Dawley Castle and Lilleshall Abbey had fallen and the focus of the fighting shifted to the south of the county where the Clubmen were active.

By November 1645 Bridgnorth, High Ercall and Ludlow were the only Royalist garrisons left in Shropshire and in the early spring of 1646 came under renewed attack. The fall of High Ercall is described In 'The Burning Bush Not Consumed' by the Puritan writer Vicars: "Having ... battered them for the space of nine hours ... by the blessing of God and our continual playing of our great shott and granadoes, which had done great execution among them, in short space we caused them to parley."

Two hundred and twelve of the garrison were allowed to depart under the terms of its surrender. Later that March, Bridgnorth fell with three hundred houses consumed by fire, as the Royalists withdrew into the castle. They held the castle until April and it was subsequently destroyed.

As Charles gave himself up to the Scots on the 5th of May, further resistance was futile and Sir Michael Woodhouse finally surrendered Ludlow the last Royalist garrison in Shropshire at the end of the month. The first Civil War had ended.

Miraculous Preservation

The Later Civil Wars and Boscobel

An eighteenth century view of the remains of Ludlow Castle, a Royalist stronghold and the last to fall to Parliament in Shropshire

The Second Civil War

In 1646 the Civil War seemed over. In Shropshire hostilities ended with the fall of Ludlow on 29th May. The same month Charles surrendered to the Scots. However, the Civil Wars were not over and Shropshire was to see two further insurrections in 1648 and 1651.

When Charles failed to agree to Scottish proposals to establish the Presbyterian Church in England they handed him over to Parliament. Held at Hampton Court, Charles continued to negotiate with Parliament, but failed to make a final agreement. As time went by the factions amongst the Parliamentary forces grew further apart. They were particularly divided as to whether the established church in England should be Presbyterian or Independent. Charles hoped to exploit such differences, expecting his enemies to turn on one another. In 1647 he escaped to Carisbrooke Castle on the Isle of Wight and subsequently agreed to a bargain with the Scots. They would support him in return for his recognition of Presbyterianism in England for three years while a permanent religious settlement was worked out. Charles would have most

of his powers restored. The Independents would be suppressed. So began what was to be called the Second Civil War in 1648 with risings in England and Wales, and a Scottish invasion. Unfortunately for the King these risings were uncoordinated and the Parliamentary army was able to defeat them.

Lord Byron returned from the continent and began to organise a Royalist insurrection in Shropshire. Various local gentlemen were also active. In Wales, Richard Scriven of Frodesley was taken prisoner at Bangor but managed to escape. During the summer of 1648 Sir Henry Lingen and Francis Ottley planned to take Ludlow and Dawley castles. The governor of Ludlow was forewarned however, and this part of the plan was thwarted. They still thought the capture of Dawley was possible and enlisted the help of a Colonel Lane, Major Eliot, Major Harcot, Parson Broughton of Wolverley, and the Giffards of Chillington, while Colonel Dudley drilled two hundred men in Boscobel Wood. Again, Parliament was equal to the threat. Some Parliamentary dragoons under the command of one Captain Janet accidentally discovered large quantities of powder and match in a field behind Parson

Broughton's house in Wolverley, Worcestershire. They also captured Major Harcot who confessed the design. The plotters were intercepted as they were about to carry out their plan. Some fled, but two were killed and eighteen were taken prisoner.

Both Dawley and Broncroft castles were dismantled after the troops had been arrested by Captain Yarrington who received the thanks of Parliament and £500. With such plots Parliamentary supporters became uneasy. Clive of Styche wrote to the Commons commenting on the lack of urgency shown by the Committee for Shropshire in raising troops. The invasion of England by the Scots army finally brought matters to a head. The Royalists were forced to show their hand as the Scots marched South. Byron planned to seize Shrewsbury and link up with Royalist forces in Wales.

Humphrey Mackworth, the Governor of Shrewsbury, was aware of this plan through an informer. The town was put into a state of readiness. The plotters planned to use the crowds as a cover at a fair on August 1st. However, many were arrested by Parliamentary troops, eighty horse having been drafted in to protect the town. A messenger who had come from Byron was captured and the whole plan was thus revealed. The Royalists hoped to rendezvous on Wattlesborough Heath at eleven

at night, proceed to Prees Heath and meet Lord Byron bringing five hundred cavalry. Thinking they would outnumber the enemy the Royalists proceeded even though they had been discovered. But Mackworth had acted before them and fifty were captured as they arrived. Others arriving heard sounds of fighting and retreated, as did those on Prees Heath. Some of them went to Wales with Byron to join the Royalist forces there. The citizens of Shrewsbury were warned against any further involvement in revolt as they witnessed the treatment of Scottish captives held in the town before transportation to the West Indies. By the end of September Parliamentary troops from Shropshire under Mytton's command were mopping up Royalist resistance in North Wales. With Mytton were the Clun preacher Vavasor Powell and John Benbow, later to play a part in the next Scots invasion of 1651. Both were wounded during an attack on Beaumaris. The war was effectively over by October 1648. Shropshire thus emerged relatively unscathed from the risings, but the triumph of Parliament had again been brought home to its inhabitants.

In London the King was held prisoner. Having fought another war because of Charles' failure to reach a settlement and his treachery in their eyes of dealing with

Broncroft Castle: Garrsioned by both sides during the wars and largely destroyed.
An original tower is now incorporated in the restored house.

Humphrey Mackworth

B.1603. d.1654. Humphrey Mackworth of Betton was the great-grandson of a notable Shrewsbury draper, John Mackworth. He can be viewed as a member of the new wealthy land owning class who owed their success to trade or the professions, rather than inheritance. A staunch Puritan, he opposed Laudian reform and from the early stages of hostilities he played an active role in opposing the King. In October 1642 he was accused of "seditious speech and action" by the King while His Majesty resided in Shrewsbury, and was charged with high treason. Avoiding capture, he was ejected from his position of Alderman in Shrewsbury and did not regain any influence in the town until its capture by Parliament in 1645.

Much to the disappointment of Thomas Mytton and the mercenary Reinking, Mackworth was appointed Governor of Shrewsbury in 1646 and he played an active role on the Parliamentary Committee for Shropshire. However, the largely Presbyterian Committee restricted his power as Governor. Mackworth was an Independent.

In August 1651, Charles II passed along the eastern border of Shropshire toward Worcester. Being informed that Mackworth was "a gentleman of an ancient house and of very different principles from those with whom his principles had ranked him", the Monarch called for the surrender of the town of Shrewsbury and an oath of loyalty. Mackworth defiantly replied, "I resolve to be found unremovable the faithfull servant of the Commonwealth of England".

Mackworth became a councillor of state to Cromwell and sat in Parliament as a Knight of the Shire in 1654. Dying in December the same year, he received a state burial in the Henry VII Chapel.

the Presbyterian Scots, the army leaders felt they could never again trust "Charles Stuart, that man of blood". The decision of the "grandees" (army council) to purge parliament of Presbyterian MPs was a clear statement of their intention. Colonel Pride was sent to expel them from the house leaving an Independent Puritan Parliament of about a hundred and forty MPs who then voted for the King's trial. The outcome was obvious and resulted in Charles' execution on 30th January 1649. Suddenly England was without a King and this revolutionary step was further compounded by the abolition of the House of Lords and Bishops and the creation of the Commonwealth, in effect 'the rump', as rulers of the state. As the army had created the rump and stood to protect them, it was they who were effectively in control.

Thus England became a revolutionary state. How much this change affected people in Shropshire is debatable. The Gentry still maintained their positions as leaders of the community. Supporters of Parliament held onto their estates. Some Royalists were not so lucky. The Newport family was almost ruined by their loyalty to the King. On the 8th February 1650, Sir Richard Newport died at Moulins in France. In his will he lamented: "By the malignity of the recent times my

family is dissolved, my chief house High Ercall, is ruined, my household stuffe and stocke sold from me, for having assisted the King."

Fines and Punishment

Sequestration (the seizure of the income from an estate) was common. This meant no livelihood or assets could be used by the owners whilst held by the Committee of Parliament for Shropshire. After the war it became possible to free one's assets by "compounding". In other words the Royalists had to declare all their assets and then receive a fine from the Committee.

Catholics, who had fought openly for the Royalist cause, and those closest to the King, were unable to "compound". Their land stayed sequestered and was eventually confiscated and sold. Some fines were so heavy that parcels of land were sold to pay off debts. The King's land was sold, as was the bishops, so there was a limited process of changing ownership during this period.

Yet there is little evidence of any real social upheaval. The Brooke family lost their land in Coalbrookdale and Madeley, but eventually regained it. In essence, the Gentry saw to it that land was sold to other gentlemen rather than aspiring craftsmen or yeomen.

Sir Francis Ottley

(1601-1649) Sir Francis Ottley was the son of Thomas Ottley of Pitchford and a descendant of a family that built its wealth upon the woollen cloth trade. Pitchford Hall stands as a monument to their fortune. Francis Ottley has been considered to be a zealous Royalist. In 1642 the King requested that Ottley raise a regiment of two hundred foot and, following this, that he should secure the town of Shrewsbury "... against all assaults, surprise, or attempt, which may bee made against the same". He was knighted for his services and appointed Governor of Shrewsbury, a post that he held until 1644. Ottley became High Sheriff of the County in 1645.

It is commonly believed that the Ottley family were secret Catholics. The mother of Francis Ottley was Mary Gifford, daughter of Roger Gifford, a physician to Elizabeth I and a known recusant. His sister Margaret married Edward Fox of the Hurst in Westbury, Shropshire, also a recusant. Interestingly, the drawing room at Pitchford Hall contains a secret hiding hole under a trap door, a common occurrence in many contemporary recusant households.

Ottley left a collection of detailed correspondence of the Royalist war effort, which provide an important source of information for historians. He appears to have been captured on three occasions at Apley House near Bridgnorth, Bridgnorth itself and also at Worcester. In addition he was forced to pay £1,200 to Parliament by the Shropshire Committee for Compounding.

Royalist Governor of Shrewsbury Sir Francis Ottley (1601-49) and family

The structure of county society remained unchanged and the Gentry retained their power.

The Ottleys were a further example of a family desperately clinging to their assets. After surrender at Bridgnorth, Sir Francis faced banishment or submission to Parliament. He chose to submit and was then subject to a large fine of £1,200. To pay it he leased the manor of Pitchford and most of his other lands. Despite his known involvement in the insurrection of 1648, when he died in 1649 his son Richard was able to redeem the estates after paying a sum of £1,400 and swearing loyalty to Parliament. Richard secretly remained an ardent Royalist and welcomed Charles II on his return in May 1660. Charles had him knighted and made Deputy Lieutenant of Shropshire. Despite their continuous support for the Royalist cause, and crypto-Catholicism, they had kept their land. From this evidence it would seem that the impact of the Civil War on Shropshire was hardly revolutionary in a social sense.

The Church, however, did undergo change. With the end of the First Civil War in 1646 Puritanism had triumphed. The Parliamentary cause embodied many different sects that increased in numbers with the lack of censorship. Parliament at first encouraged Presbyterianism as the official state church. Presbyterianism was Calvinist in its origins. It was against bishops. Power came from congregations, administered by presbyteries at parish level, with diocesan synods and a national assembly above them. In Scotland, Presbyterianism had been adopted after the Reformation in 1560.

Many MPs were Presbyterian in outlook and favoured its introduction as the state church. Other MPs, known as Independents, argued that each congregation should be able to decide on its own form of Protestant worship. The Westminster Assembly of 1643 pledged to establish Presbyterianism in England by accepting the Solemn League and Covenant, abolishing bishops, the prayer book and traditional services. The process was effectively begun at the end of the war in 1646 so that by April 1647, Shropshire was organised into six presbyteries and ministers appointed that accepted the new system. Those who did not were horribly treated, as in the case of Andrew Bailey, the vicar of Shifnal. In his account of the "Sufferings of the Clergy", Walker wrote of Bailey:

"They not only Turned him out of his Living, but Sequestered his Temporal Estate (though he had then a Wife and 16 Children) Plundered him, and Burnt his Books, to the Value of 300 pounds and carried away at one time in Plate and Goods, to the Value of 500 pounds. They also Turned some of the Children out of Bed, flung the Feathers about the House, and made Bags of the Tickings to carry away what Goods they could put in them: And a party of Horse being sent from Stafford to Apprehend Mr. Baily, not finding him, they Threatened to put lighted Matches betwixt the Fingers of one of his Children, who was not Ten Years old, in order to extort from him a Confession where his Father was. But though Providence preserved him at that time, after he fell into their Hands, and was Twice imprisoned."

However, by December 1648 with Pride's Purge (The removal from Parliament of MPs who supported Presbyterianism by the Army Council who were largely Independents), the situation was changing. Thus Congregationalism prevailed. Not really a separate

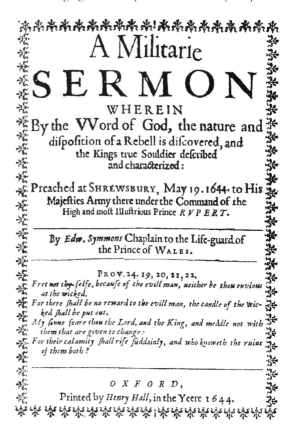

A Royalist military sermon preached at Shrewsbury used to promote anti-Parliament propaganda

Vavasor Powell

B.1617 d.1670. Although he was born in Wales, Vavasour Powell spent his formative years in south-west Shropshire. Isaac Thomas, an innkeeper and mercer of Bishop's Castle employed him as a groom. At the age of seventeen Powell was sent to Oxford by his uncle, Erasmus Powell vicar of Clun. He did not complete his education at Oxford and returned to Shropshire where he acted as curate to his uncle and then as a schoolmaster in Clun. During the period 1638-9 Powell was greatly influenced by Puritan thinkers. In the second Civil War of 1648 he received a bullet wound while on a preaching mission to Parliamentary forces at Anglesey whereupon he claimed to have heard a voice from heaven saying "I have chosen thee to preach the gospel". He became an itinerant preacher and was known as a republican and fifth monarchist. Despite being active in ejecting many of the Welsh clergy opposed to the Commonwealth from their livings, Powell opposed the rule of Oliver Cromwell as Lord Protector. He was repeatedly arrested and eventually imprisoned at Shrewsbury in 1660 for nine weeks. During the restoration he refused to declare his allegiance to the King and continued his unauthorised preaching. He was known to have preached a single sermon lasting seven hours. His continued disobedience led to his arrest and he died in prison.

Vavasor Powell provides an example of a radical free-thinker. Baxter described Powell as "an honest injudicious zealot". His cousin Jeremiah Powell was among the leaders of the Clubman movement in south-west Shropshire.

denomination, it effectively described Protestant congregations who rejected the notion of a state church. Congregationalists or Independents had many different opinions, but all agreed that churches should be able to organise themselves and join in any association as long as it was not imposed on them - or Catholic of course. It had no hard and fast theology and so those that had been Anglican priests before could continue in their livings as long as they swore the oath of allegiance to the Republic known as the Engagement.

Clergy, who refused to take the oath, were ejected and so continued the pattern of "coming and going" which blighted many parishes in Shropshire. In Pontesbury, for example, Ralph Morhall had been appointed in 1645 to succeed the sequestered Samuel Greaves. Then, Morhall was himself ejected and replaced by Andrew Warter. The concept of a one church state was eroded. The idea that a range of denominations could co-exist was implanted throughout the shires. In this respect the Interregnum did prove revolutionary.

Charles II and Boscobel

Royalist resistance was still not over, however, and Shropshire was to be the scene of one final drama that marked the end of the Civil Wars. With the execution of Charles I, his eldest son Charles now claimed the title of King. Charles arrived from exile in the spring of 1650,

and having signed the Presbyterian covenant, was able to gain considerable Scottish support. When Cromwell defeated his followers at Dunbar in September, Charles, in a desperate gamble, invaded England in August 1651 marching south towards London. He was intercepted by Cromwell at Worcester on the 3rd September where his army of twelve thousand was defeated by a larger Parliamentary force.

Charles' army disintegrated and became fugitives as they fled northwards. The Earl of Derby and the Earl of Lauderdale, together with some officers, were captured near Newport, Shropshire. The Earl of Cleveland stayed ahead of his pursuers for three weeks and took refuge at Woodcote near Newport until he too was captured. Lord Talbot, on the other hand, did manage to escape capture as he fled to the family seat at Longford where he hid in an outbuilding. Ordinary soldiers were less fortunate. Hundreds were captured in and around the County, including two hundred near Shifnal. Some were housed in St Giles Church, Shrewsbury. Local accounts note: "1651. Payd John Smith for makeinge cleane S. Giles Church after the Scots ... 2s 0d." Many were transported to Barbados.

Charles himself escaped from Worcester on Wednesday 3rd September and rode north accompanied by a large group of his noble companions. The implications of defeat were severe. As Parliament had executed his

King Charles II famously linked with Boscobel and its oak tree after his flight from Worcester in 1651

father it was certain that he would suffer the same fate if caught. Where was his best chance of escape and how should he travel? In an account of his escape dictated to Samuel Pepys, Charles remembered:

"At last we got about sixty that were gentlemen and officers, and slipt away out of the high-road that goes to Lancastershire . . . for it was then too late for us to get to London, on horse-back, riding directly for it, nor could we do it, because there was yet many people of quality with us that I could not get rid of".

They rode through Stourbridge and on, through enemy troops who failed to challenge them, to Kinver Heath. At some point Lord Derby suggested Boscobel as a hiding place, but on the advice of Charles Giffard who was related to the owner of Boscobel, they arrived on the morning of the 4th at White Ladies, a house attached to the remains of a 12th century Augustinian Priory. Charles' story continued:

"We went that night about twenty miles, to a place called White Ladies, hard by Tong-Castle, by the

advice of Mr Giffard, where we stopped, and got some little refreshment of bread and cheese, such as we could get, it being the beginning of the day. This White Ladies was a private house that Mr Giffard, who was a Staffordshire man, had told me belonged to honest people that lived thereabouts".

The owner of the house Frances Cotton (born a Giffard and now a widow) was not in residence, but her servants, the Penderel family, were. It was they who effectively concealed Charles and saved him from capture and death. The Penderel family consisted of the mother Joan and six sons, one of whom had been transported to Barbados, having fought for Charles I. Two lived at White Ladies, John and George, Humphrey at a local corn mill, Richard at Hobbal Grange with his mother and William at Boscobel. They were Catholics like their landlords. These were farm workers not gentry, unable to read and write but certainly loyal to the Royalist cause.

Charles' retinue now divided, with Charles having decided to remain at White Ladies while others planned to join other Royalist troops in an attempt to head for Scotland. Charles' shrewd analysis of the situation, and his single mindedness in saving his own neck, become apparent in his narrative. It gives the reader a fascinating insight into the mind of the future King.

> "There came a country-fellow, that told us, there were three thousand of our horse just hard by Tong Castle, upon the heath, all disorder, under David Leslie, and some other of the general officers: upon which there were some of the people of quality that were with me, who were very earnest that I should go to him and endeavour to go to Scotland; which I thought was absolutely impossible, knowing very well that the country would all rife upon us, and that men who had deserted me when they were in good order, would never stand to me when they have been beaten."

Charles wisely decided to head for London instead of Scotland as Leslie's army was routed near Newport. He adopted a disguise by wearing ordinary clothes and cutting his hair short. After the others had left Charles hid in a wood with Richard Penderel, recalling:

> "He was a Roman Catholic, and I chose to trust them, because I knew they had hiding holes for priests, that I thought I might make use of in case of need. ... In this wood I staid all day, without meat or drink; and by great good fortune it rained all the time, which hindered them, as I believe, from coming into the wood to search for men that might be fled thither."

Charles then began to change his plans. He decided to attempt to escape over the Severn into Wales and then to Swansea and on to France by boat.

> "So that night, as soon as it was dark, Richard Pendrell and I took our journey on foot towards the Severn, intending to pass over a ferry, halfway between Bridgnorth and Shrewsbury. But as we were going in the night, we came by a mill where I heard some people talking, ... and as we conceived it was about twelve or one o'clock at night, and the country-fellow desired me not to answer if any body should ask me any questions, because I had not the accent of the country.
>
> Just as we came to the mill [Evelith], we could see the miller, as I believed, sitting at the mill door, he being in white cloathes, it being very dark at night. he called out, "Who goes there?" Upon which Richard Penderell answered,

The Penderel family, William, on the left, Richard, on the right, who risked their lives to help hide Charles II at Boscobel and ensure his 'miraculous preservation'

Ruins of Shrawardine Castle destroyed in the war, situated close to the River Severn on the Shropshire-Wales border

The bust of Gervase Needham inside Bishop's Castle church, clergyman and a Clubmen leader

Lea Castle: Once a Royalist garrison, its ruins now form part of a farmhouse

Madeley: The barn that sheltered Charles II during his flight from the Battle of Worcester

Madeley: Close up of the plaque on the barn that sheltered Charles II

The grave of John Benbow (executed in 1651), Old St Chad's churchyard, Shrewsbury

Moreton Corbet Castle: A Royalist Garrison later captured and dismantled by Parliament. Its ruins can still be viewed today.

Myddle: The source for Richard Gough's chronicles of village life in the seventeenth century, The History of Myddle.

"Neighbours going home," or some such like words. Whereupon the miller cried out, "If you be neighbours, stand or I will knock you down." Upon which, we believing there was company in the house, the fellow bade me follow him close, and he run a gate that went up a dirty lane, up a hill, and opening the gate, the miller cried out, "Rogues! rogues!" and thereupon some men came out of the mill after us, which I believed was Soldiers: so we fell a running, both of us, up the lane, as long as we could run, it being very deep, and very dirty, till at last I bade him leap over a hedge, and lye still to hear if anybody followed us; which we did, and continued lying down upon the ground about half an hour, when, hearing nobody come, we continued our way on to the village [Madeley] upon the Severn; where the fellow told me there was an honest gentleman, one Mr Woolfe, that lived in that town, where I might be with great safety ...

Mr Woolfe, when the country-fellow told him that it was one that had escaped from the battle of Worcester, said, that for his part, it was so dangerous a thing to harbour any body that was known, that he would not venture his neck for any man, unless it were the King himself. Upon which, Richard Penderell, very indiscreetly, and without any leave, told him that it was I. Upon which Mr Woolfe replied, that he should be very ready to venture all he had in the world to secure me. Upon which Richard Penderell came and told me what he had done at which I was a little troubled, but then there was no remedy, the day being just coming on, and I must either venture that, or run some greater danger."

As dawn came, Charles entered the house and was told by Mr Woolfe that Parliament had troops stationed in Madeley and a guard at the ferry. Woolfe hid him in the barn rather than the priest holes in the house, presumably because the soldiers already knew the holes. Finding the crossing of the Severn blocked he resolved to return to Boscobel.

"So we set out as soon as it was dark. But, as we came by the mill again, we had no mind to be questioned a second time there; and therefore asking Richard Penderell, whether he could swim or no? and how deep the river was? He told me, it was a scurvy river, not easy to pass in places, and that he could not swim. So I told him, that the river being but a little one, I would help him over. Upon which we went over some closes to the riverside, and I entering the river first, to see whether I could myself go over, who knew how to swim, found it was but a little above my middle; and thereupon taking Richard Penderell by the hand I helped him over."

On their return they discovered another fugitive being sheltered by the Penderels, Major William Careless, a local Catholic. It was decided that the safest hiding place for the coming day, Saturday the sixth, would be to hide in a large and bushy oak tree in the wood, which surrounded the house.

"He (Careless) told me ... that he knew but one way how to pass the next day, and that was, to get up into a great oak, in a pretty plain place, where we might see round about us; for the enemy would certainly search at the wood for people that had made their escape. Of which proposition of his I approving, we (that is to say, Careless and I) went, and carried up with us some victuals for the whole day, viz. bread, cheese, small beer, and nothing else, and got up into a great oak, that had been lopt some three or four years before, and being grown out again, very bushy and thick, could not be seen through, and here we staid all day. I having, in the meantime, sent Penderell's brother to Mr Pitchcroft's, to know whether my Lord Wilmot was there or no; and had word brought me by him, at night, that my Lord was there; that there was a very secure hiding-hole in Mr Pitchcroft's house, and that he desired me to come hither to him ... while we were in this tree we see soldiers going up and down, in the thicket of the wood, searching for persons escaped, we seeing them, now and then, peeping out of the wood."

In the evening Charles having had enough of the tree went back into the house and decided to stay there overnight. 'Boscobel', by Thomas Blount, a Catholic lawyer from Worcester, was published in 1660 and gives an alternative account of the King's movements. It contradicts the King's account in places, notably as to the events of that Saturday night. Other writers such as Whitgreave, the owner of nearby Moseley Old Hall in Staffordshire, which Charles was to visit next, also agree with Blount that the king stayed at Boscobel overnight. Blount says:

"That night the Good-wife ... provided some chickens for His Majesties supper ... and a little Pallet was put into the secret place for His Majesty

A seventeenth century illustration showing Charles II hiding in the oak tree at Boscobel

to rest in; some of the Brothers being continually upon duty watching the Avenues of the house and the Road-way, to prevent dangerous surprise."

There seems little doubt that Charles was hidden in the priest hole at the top of the stairs, on the second floor of Boscobel. The stairs lead into a gallery where cheeses were stored and the whole floorboard would have been taken up and nailed back down once the King was inside. With cheeses and straw covering the floor this would conceal the hiding place well, both visually and in terms of smell, from the possible use of tracker dogs. In the event the soldiers hunting Charles did not arrive and the next day after praying in the upper gallery, which contained a concealed Catholic chapel, and sitting in the garden, he left in the evening on a carthorse to Moseley Old Hall.

From Moseley he was transferred to Bentley Hall where he was disguised as a servant and accompanying Jane Lane made his way south to Bristol. Failing to find a boat that could take him he was eventually carried to France from Shoreham in Sussex having spent some time trying to find a suitable point of departure on the south coast.

Charles was lucky not to be found at Boscobel. Not only did he avoid capture whilst in the oak tree but he also narrowly missed a visit to the house by soldiers. Blount gives the following account:

> "Being come to Whiteladies, on Tuesday, they called for Mr George Giffard, who lived in an apartment of the house, present a pistol to his breast, and bad him confess where the King was, or he should presently die; ... They used the like threats and violence (mingled notwithstanding with high promises of reward) to Mrs. Anne Andrew ... they searched every corner of the house, broke down much of the Wainscoat, and at last beat the Intelligencer (Cornet) severely, for making them lose their labours."

Charles was certainly grateful on his restoration in 1660. In 1664 the King granted numerous rents to the Penderel family. In total, the annuities added up to the following per annum:

Granted to Ric. Pendrill and Mary his wife.	£100	0	0
To Wm. Pendrill & Jone his wife.	£100	0	0
To Jo. Pendrill.	£ 66	33	4
To Hump. Pendrill.	£ 66	33	4
To George Pendrill.	£ 66	33	4
To Widow Yates for her Life.	£ 50	0	0

Francis Yates, who had escorted the King from Kinver Heath, was later executed for his part in the escape. His widow thus appears in the list of annuities. Their descendants still receive money today.

Had Charles been caught he would certainly have been killed. His father had suffered death having instigated the Second Civil War. His son's attempt in 1651 could hardly have been looked upon mercifully by the Rump Parliament engaged in "Godly rule".

Boscobel has thus achieved great status as the place where the British monarchy was saved. Charles II planted acorns in Hyde Park, which came from the tree in which he had hidden. The story is also remembered by the famous inn tabard "The Royal Oak", of which there are hundreds in Britain commemorating the event, including one close to Boscobel at Bishop's Wood. Boscobel itself became a celebrated tourist attraction and the oak that had sheltered Charles an obvious target for souvenir hunters. William Stukeley in 1712 described the tree as "almost cut away by travellers". Today a descendant of the original tree protected by a metal fence is the only survivor of the wood that once surrounded Boscobel. Other trees also exist throughout the world, as far afield as Japan, grown from Boscobel acorns.

Visitors to Boscobel usually find the King's story a romantic one. This encourages a sympathetic bias towards the fugitive underdog Charles. However, there is another side to the story. In Parliamentary eyes, Charles had simply plunged the country into another bloody struggle and had caused the deaths of further hundreds of people in an attempt to regain the throne, without any indication that he would prove any more reasonable than his father. From their point of view, he deserved to die for his treasonable attack on the new 'Godly' Republic.

The Last Uprisings

During the years after 1651 various Shropshire gentry were involved in plots against the governments of the Interregnum outside the County. Within Shropshire a plan to seize Shrewsbury Castle in March 1654 by Sir Thomas Harris of Boreatton and Ralph Kynaston was foiled. Intelligence of the plot was obtained by Colonel Humphrey Mackworth, Junior, now Governor of Shrewsbury, who quickly acted to surprise Harris and his fellow conspirators. The story is recounted by one John Evanson of Shrewsbury, who took part in the action:

John Benbow

B.1623 d.1651. John Benbow was the son of William Benbow a tanner living in Mardol, Shrewsbury. During the first Civil War Benbow was instrumental in the taking of Shrewsbury by Parliament in February 1645. During the early morning he led a company of troopers from the end of Castle Foregate through some fields to the castle ditch next to the River Severn. He then led his party up the bank and using scaling ladders climbed the castle wall. This enabled him to open the gates at St. Mary's Water Lane and Reinking then entered the town with ease. Having resided in Shrewsbury, he had a first hand knowledge of the layout of the town's defences. Whether or not his action was treacherous is another matter. We do not know whether he deserted from the Royalists or whether he already owed allegiance to Parliament.

In 1648 he was fighting at Beaumauris in Wales with Vavasour Powell on the side of Parliament, but by 1651 Benbow had changed sides and was a commander in the army of Charles II. He was captured after the battle of Worcester and taken to Chester where he was tried by a Parliamentary court under the presidency of Sir Humphrey Mackworth. Benbow was sentenced to death and subsequently taken to Shrewsbury where he was shot. His execution took place in the "cabbage garden" beneath the Castle Mount near to the Council House. This was the same spot where he had led a party of Parliamentary soldiers over the town wall six years earlier. Benbow was buried in old St. Chad's churchyard and his headstone can still be seen today. It says:

"Here lieth the body of Captaine John Benbow who was buried October ye 16. 1651."

It is likely that a namesake, Thomas Benbow, who may have been a relative and fought alongside John Benbow at Worcester, is also recorded as being shot at Shrewsbury four days after his execution.

Benbow is an example of someone who paid the ultimate price for changing sides. Many people transferred their allegiance during the period as events developed, because of religious or political beliefs. Having supported Parliament throughout the war, they found themselves in opposition to the Commonwealth. We do not know why Benbow fought for Charles II. It may have been that he disagreed with the execution of the King, as many other people did at the time, believing that things had gone too far.

"After some opposition we seized him (Harris) and seven others, the rest escaping through by-ways, and brought them to Shrewsbury, whence he was sent to London and committed to the Tower."

In the confused climate following the death of Oliver Cromwell in 1658 and deposition of his son Richard Cromwell on 25th May 1659, several Royalist conspiracies were aborted before they were carried out due to intelligence reports. On the 30th January 1660, Captain Thomas Hill wrote to Parliament:

"Shrewsbury Castle. Upon ye 27th this castle was betrayed by a ... party of Cavaliers ... I then privately strengthened the garrison with our men that were without, and with a commanded party marched out that night and apprehended some of those concerned in the plot, whom I have sent to our Governor, from whom you will receive them. I desire the sense of the House as to the disposal of the persons now in custody."

One of the "Cavaliers" was Sir Thomas Middleton who during the first Civil War had fought for Parliament. Many such men now welcomed the return of Charles II, who having issued the declaration of Breda guaranteeing various pardons and freedom from reprisals, returned from exile and was proclaimed King on the 8th May 1660. An entry in the parish register for Shrawardine, 29th May 1660 (though seemingly added at a later date) declared:

"His gracious majesty our dread sovereign, king Charles the second, came to London the 29th of this Month, attended with the greatest part of the Nobilitie & Gentrye of the land, where with all demonstrations of joy, he was welcomed and received. Never was more cordial love & honour showed to any king than was to this exiled prince, at his reception into the kingdom in all places."

The Civil War in Shropshire was well and truly ended.

The Misery of War
The Effects of War on Shropshire Civilians

Financing the war

It would be a mistake to view the war as a military conflict that was separate from the lives of those who were non-combatants. The war had a massive impact on civilians and touched the majority of people's lives in one way or another. Richard Baxter observed, "I think there were few parishes where at one time or other blood had not been shed".

One of the most important reasons why Parliament eventually won the war was their greater efficiency in gathering finances for the war effort. The Royalists depended on finance raised through contributions, sequestrations (confiscation of property), loans and excise. At first this did not seem to present a great problem. Clarendon states with reference to the King's troops entering Shrewsbury in 1642 that "the Soldiers behaved themselves orderly, and people were not inclined, or provoked to complain of their new Guests; and the remainder of the Plate ... supplied the present necessary Expenses very conveniently."

Clarendon's assessment, however, belies the initial difficulties in obtaining revenue from the town. An assessment of £500 was "ordered for his Majesty's Service", a month's pay for "120 soldiers" for a garrison in the town, £140 for fortifications and "£17 to the King's Princes and Dukes, Footmen and Trumpeters". But the corporation could not meet such demands easily. A petition was drawn to "show the weak Estate of the Town, and to desire a week longer to raise money for his Majesty's Necessity".

Other more dubious methods of gathering finance were not beyond Charles. The King accepted a donation of £6,000 from Sir Francis Newport in return for a peerage for his father Sir Richard Newport who became Baron Newport of High Ercall, while Richard Gough recalled that Sir Thomas Lister presented Charles with a purse of gold and the King knighted him. The King also obtained money from Catholics who sent their recusancy fines in advance. This was obtained secretly by letter and brought the Monarch as much as £5,000.

The Newport Family

The Newport family of High Ercall were staunch Royalists. The head of the family, Richard Newport (1587-1651), after some reluctance, supported the King and helped to finance the war effort.

The eldest son, Francis Newport (1619-1708), followed his father into the House of Parliament. He was returned as MP for Shrewsbury in the Short Parliament of 1640 and received notoriety for his support of the ill-fated Lord Strafford, the King's adviser, who was condemned by The House.

The heir to the Newport estate wasted little time in declaring for the King at the outbreak of hostilities and joined Charles at Oxford in January 1643-4. He was captured during the siege of Oswestry in 1644 and remained a prisoner until March 1647-8. Fortunes fluctuated as he succeeded to his father's estate in 1651. On the 9th June 1655 he was arrested and committed to the Tower under suspicion of engaging in a Royalist plot. After his release he was re-arrested in 1656-7 being involved in an attempt to take Shrewsbury Castle. On his restoration, Charles II granted Shrewsbury Castle and demesne to Francis Newport. Holding various Royal offices, he was eventually created Viscount Newport of Bradford in Shropshire in March 1675.

More intrigue surrounds Andrew Newport (1623-1699), the second son of Francis Newport. In a work of apparent fiction by Defoe, Andrew Newport is identified as the subject of the "Memoirs of a Cavalier". In the 1792 edition the book is entitled "Memoirs of Colonel Andrew Newport." In the book Newport claimed to have fought as a mercenary in Europe, after his father suggested that he go abroad as "a private gentleman, a scholar, or as a soldier". During the Civil War, he supposedly fought for the King.

Historians are unable to agree on the authenticity of the work, but from what is known about the early life of Andrew Newport it is unlikely that he ever fought as a mercenary in Europe or took part in the Civil War. However, there is no doubt over his Royalist activities during the Commonwealth. In 1657 he was treasurer for money secretly collected by Royalists for Charles II, opposed the cautious approach adopted by the "Sealed Knot" (a secret society dedicated to restoring the monarchy during the Protectorate and which has now lent its name to a Civil War re-enactment society) and was involved in the failed Royalist uprising in 1659. In that year Charles II wrote: "I desire that Andrew Newport, upon whose affection and ability to serve me I do very much depend ... may be put in mind to do all he can for the possessing of Shrewsbury."

Andrew Newport had a successful political career during the reign of Charles II, sitting as MP for Montgomeryshire. Between 1689-1698 the town of Shrewsbury returned him to Parliament. Together with the elevation of his brother Francis Newport, this was a remarkable change in fortune for a family whose prospects looked bleak at the end of the first Civil War. Their estates had been sequestrated, but as impoverished as the Newports appeared, they were to be sufficiently rewarded for their loyalty on the restoration of Charles II.

Such methods were fine at the outset, but as the war dragged on they proved inadequate to produce the revenue that by contrast Parliament was able to raise. Parliament adopted a programme of high taxation that was paradoxically similar to that which they had rebelled against when levied by the King in the form of ship money. In 1642 they drew up an Act of Parliament (known as the Act of £400,000) to raise money nationally. This was followed in 1643 by a series of weekly and monthly assessments, sequestrations, compulsory loans and excise.

In addition, an Act of 22 December 1642 ordered that those clergy who joined the King's army should be "sequestrated of the profits of their livings". Where such proceedings could not be used other, more severe, action was taken. Garbett claimed:

"The Round Heads of Wem was a name of terror. They extended their ravages far, and were very troublesome to the Royalists, imprisoning their bodies, and sequestrating their estates. Richard Sandland's house in the Noble street was their prison. They drove doctor Midcalf from the rectory of Wem, John Arnway from that of Hodnet, and James Fleetwood from the vicarage of Prees."

The growing cost of war led Royalists to demand forced loans. As early as April 1643, Lord Capel attempted to exact money from all "persons of substance" in Shrewsbury. He also required them to supply soldiers. The town's Corporation eventually compromised by giving £500 with a guarantee of more money in the future. In January 1644 the corporation voted to give a further £1000 but this was never paid in full.

If all other methods of raising money and materials failed there was always ransom. Despite having previously given the King a considerable contribution to the war effort, Humphrey Walcot was held prisoner by the Royalist garrison of Ludlow. Walcot was not released until he agreed to make further large payment.

After the capitulation of Oswestry, the local Corporation was forced to provide the Parliamentary army with £500 to prevent plunder, an activity that was increasing throughout the County. On the 24th February 1645 the Committee for Shropshire, now residing in Shrewsbury, wrote to William Brereton:

"We feel very much the misery of war, which is destruction and dissolution, if not timely prevented. We did partly foresee the likelihood of plundering and to that end acquainted Col. Bowyer that, if the town might be kept from plunder, we would raise £2,000..."

Civilian disruption

Looting increased, as the war became more bitter and protracted. In March 1644 Apley Castle was taken by Parliament. The head of the household, Mr Hamner, was taken prisoner and £1,500 of his goods were taken. Further indignity followed as the Royalists under

Sir William Vaughan and a Colonel Ellis recaptured the castle a few days later and seized the remainder of his goods to the value of £3,000-£4,000. A survey of the Bridgewater estates in 1650 noted that Richard Matthews of New Marton "had lost all by the wars" while John Tonna had "not a ragg left."

At times such plunder appeared to be indiscriminate. It was not uncommon to suffer at the hands of the side to whom loyalty had been shown. During the summer of 1644, the Shrewsbury Corporation complained that despite their compliance with the Royalist garrison situated in the town, "most of their horses were stolen from them by the soldiers".

Civilians also had to billet soldiers and fit them out. In 1645 this had cost the town of Ludlow alone £850 17s 10d. In Bridgnorth the inhabitants were initially asked to provide the King's soldiers with an allowance of 2s 6d per day. The accounts of the Bridgnorth Corporation also show that individuals had to be reimbursed for the expense of keeping soldiers in the town. £4 was paid to Thomas Glover "towardes his losses in horses, bridles, and sadles, and swordes, for setting forth of dragoones for his Majesties service". When the town of Shrewsbury was required to increase the funding of the local garrison in 1644, the inhabitants were quick to point out that "they were promised that no free quarter should be put on them". Such promises were easily broken.

An army also had to be fed and garrisons made heavy demands upon the surrounding countryside.

In 1644, over eighty receipts for provisions received from the Liberties of Shrewsbury show that the garrisons consumed a wide range of foodstuffs. They included cheese and butter from Harlescott and Grinshill; "Delivered out of Hencott" were cheese, rye, butter and bacon; and large quantities of similar produce, as well as oats and barley, came from places such as Battlefield, Hadnall and Hanwood.

Towns faced extra costs where they had to prepare themselves for attack. In Bridgnorth, those citizens who were unable to provide a labourer to work on the town's fortifications were forced to pay a levy of 6d per day. Such costs did not just affect those inside a town. In 1643 people living outside the walls of Ludlow were ordered to erect a fence or rampart 45 inches high and 36 inches thick, by Whitsun, for the defence of the town.

The death of soldiers affected the communities from which they came, leaving widows, orphans and dependants to fend for themselves. In Colemere an estate survey described a Mrs Davies as "a poor widow her husband killed at Montgomery fight". Soldiers who had been skilled members of communities left gaps, which had an effect upon the economy. Between 1640-50 admissions of masters to the Shearman's craft in Shrewsbury stood at just 38 compared with 61 a decade earlier.

Many civilians were killed during the fighting. This was more likely in sieges when artillery bombardment and fire made death a distinct

Cornett Collins

The tale of the soldier Cornett Collins is told in Richard Gough's History of Myddle:

"There happened noe considerable act of hostility in this parish during the time of the warres, save only one small skirmish, in Myddle, part of which I saw, while I was a school boy att Myddle, under Mr Richard Rodericke, who commanded us boys to come into the church, soe that wee could not see the whole action, but it was thus. There was one Cornett Collins, an Irishman, who was a Garrison soldier for the King, at Shrawardine Castle. This Collins made excursions very often into this parish, and took away Cattle, provision, and bedding, and what he pleased. On the day before this conflict, hee had been att Myddle taking away bedding, and when Margaret, the wife of Allen Chaloner, the Smith, had brought out and showed him her best bed, hee thinking it too coarse, cast it into the lake, before the door, and trod it under his horse's feet. This Cornett, on the day that this contest happened, came to Myddle and seven soldiers with him, and his horse having cast a shoe, hee alighted att Allen Chaloner's Shop to have a new one put on.

There was one Richard Maning, a Garrison soldier at Morton Corbett, for the Parliament. This Maning was brought up as a servant under Thomas Jukes, of Newton, with whom hee lived many years, and finding that Nat. Owen, (of whom I spoak before,) did trouble this neighbourhood, hee had a grudge against him, and came with seven more soldiers with him, hoping to find Owen att Myddle with his wife. This Maning and his companions came to Webscott, and soe over Myddle Parke, and came into Myddle att the gate by Mr. Gittin's house att what time the Cornett's horse was a shoeing. The Cornett hearing the gate clap, looked by the end of the shop and saw soldiers coming, and thereupon hee, and his men mounted their horses; and as the Cornett came att the end of the shop, a brisk young fellow shott him throw the body with a carbine shott, and hee fell down in the lake att Allen Challoner's door. His men fled, two were taken, and as Maning was pursuing them in Myddle wood Field, which was then uninclosed, Maning having the best horse overtook them, while his partners were far behind, but one of the Cornett's men shott Maning's horse which fell down dead under him, and Maning had been taken prisoner had not some of his men came to rescue him. Hee took the saddle under his arm, and the bridle in his hand, and went the next way to Wem, which was then a garrison for the Parliament. The horse was killed on a bank near the further side of Myddle field, where the widow Mansell has now a piece inclosed. The Cornett was carried into Allen Chaloner's house, and laid on the floor; hee desired to have a bed laid under him, butt Margaret told him, she had none but that which hee saw yesterday; hee prayed her to forgive him, and lay that under him, which she did.

Mr Rodericke was sent for to pray for him. I went with him, and saw the Cornett lying on the bed, and much blood running along the floor. In the night following, a Troop of horse came from Shrawardine, and pressed a team in Myddle, and soe took the Cornett to Shrawardine, where hee dyed the next day."

Gough was a schoolboy when he witnessed this traumatic incident. Many similar acts of violence intruded into the lives of ordinary civilians trying to maintain their normal way of life, and affected many more people than has sometimes been imagined.

The story is interesting on a number of levels. Collins is an example of one of the many Irish soldiers that were brought over by the Royalists to swell the ranks of their army. They were feared because of their Catholicism and association with the Ulster massacres of 1641. The tale is in itself a piece of mild anti-Catholic propaganda, singling Collins out as a looter. Interestingly enough, Gough's moral anecdote presents the Protestant Margaret Challoner in a compassionate light, being able to forgive "the Cornett" despite his wrongdoing.

It also shows us that looting was a common feature of the war and the petty level on which it was sometimes carried out. Not only did they take goods and possessions, garrisons often relied upon local communities for unpaid services such as horse shoeing and repairs, which was a further drain on the local community.

Myddle was in the unfortunate position of being in between Parliamentary and Royalist garrisons (as many villages were). Both sides attempted to exert control over as many settlements as they could in order to gather provisions and taxes, without necessarily stationing troops in them. This minor example illustrates how the war was often one of attrition, with small conflicts improving the tactical position of one side or another.

The account also gives the historian a picture of the primitive medical provision at the time. Having suffered gun shot wounds to the body, there was virtually no treatment available and Collins was effectively left to bleed to death.

Finally this tale presents us with a snapshot of human jealousy and sexual intrigue. Richard Maning suspected that Nathaniel Owen was having an affair with his wife. The disruption that the war caused and the movement of troops up and down the country provided excitement and new experiences for even the remotest communities.

possibility. A besieging army entering a town with the prospect of plunder was a terrifying experience for the inhabitants. While under siege from Parliamentary troops, the Royalist garrison set fire to the town of Bridgnorth whilst withdrawing into the castle. Bellet noted:

> "The misery of the inhabitants is described as having been most severe. Rich and poor alike ... were left houseless, and sought shelter where they could, in the fields around the town, in thickets, and under rocks: all their property destroyed, and their life itself in jeopardy. Many a wretched invalid ... would be forgotten, and left to die a more awful death than they looked for - their own bed becoming their funeral pile."

Disease followed armies and also took its toll on the civilian population. Plague and typhus were the most common. As plague was not uncommon during the seventeenth century it is not always possible to attach outbreaks of the disease to war. However, the disruption of civilian diet and contact with a large number of potential carriers undoubtedly increased the incidence of disease. In 1642 burials in St. Chad's, Shrewsbury were sixty percent above the average, while in the parish of St. Alkmund they rose by two-thirds. Some people met their end in more unlikely ways. An entry in the register for St. Mary's Parish, Shrewsbury, 1645, records: " Mr Edwards, a divine who was slaine by a Chamber peece breakeinge in the Castle the 29th of July at the rejoyceinge for a greate victory obtayned in the west by the Parliament, buried."

People who lived and worked in a garrisoned town, but were loyal to the outside enemy, also had to tread carefully. In Ludlow on the 21st May 1643, a warrant to arrest Richard Walker was issued "on suspicion of carrying letters to Brampton Bryan Castle". Other messengers were more cunning than the unfortunate Walker. Richard Clarke of Myddle Wood was by all accounts "naturally ingeneous". Richard Gough reluctantly conceded as much when writing that:

> "Hee had a smooth way of flattering discourse, and was a perfect master in the art of dissembling. Hee was listed for a soldier on the Parliament in Wem, whilst hee was yet but a mere boy. There was nothing in manhood or valor in him, and yet hee was serviceable

to the officers of that Garrison by carrying of letters to theire friends, and correspondents that were in Garrisons of the adverse party. Hee had an old ragged coate on purpose which hee would putt on, and goe as a beggar boy. Hee carried a short stick, such as boys call, a dog staffe. There was a hole boared in the end of it, and there the letters were putt, and a pegge after them, and that end hee putt in dirt. If hee met with soldiers, hee would throw his sticke at birds, soe that it might goe over the hedge, and then goe over to fetch it. When hee came to the Garrison, hee would begg from door to door, and consort himself with beggars until hee came to the place where he was to deliver his letter."

War also had a direct impact upon trade. The need for military control of the River Severn disrupted traditional river traffic and those communities such as Shrewsbury and Bridgnorth that relied heavily upon it. Military garrisons along the Severn such as those at Atcham, Benthall, Buildwas and Montford Bridge effectively strangled the passage of free trade. The everyday trade of local communities also suffered where nearby garrisons could effect quick raids to secure supplies, prevent food and materials reaching the enemy, or simply attempt to undermine the resolve of townspeople and villagers. The accounts of the bailiff of the Bridgewater estates in the Ellesmere area recorded: "I Arthur Swanwick was driven from ye Lodge farm plundered by ye Kings forces and lost of Corne Cattell and Housholde Stuffe at least 200 s. worth and God knowe whether ever I shall enjoy a foote of it againe".

Consequently these and similar incidents throughout the county led to large rental arrears and unpaid tithes. Markets and fairs particularly suffered from the attentions of soldiers from both sides. On 7 August 1644 Mytton and some of his men came within three miles of the town of Shrewsbury via Meole and Atcham Bridge and "drove away many horses, calves and sheep belonging to Governor Hunckes; besides greatly inconveniencing a fair that was being held in the town that day."

As the war became prolonged the combined effects of billeting, taxation and looting provoked ordinary people into challenging the authority of local officers in charge and, in effect, to challenge the notion of traditional authority. In addition to the activities of

clubmen in south-west Shropshire, there is evidence
of some resistance to demands for money in Shifnal
where Royalist soldiers were wounded and kept
prisoner as they attempted to collect arrears of the
King's levy. In Much Wenlock the mercenary Van
Byrusch complained to Prince Rupert that the
inhabitants "almost rise against me".

The challenge to authority

With the removal of the monarchy, the abolition
of the Lords and Bishops, and the creation of
a republic, traditional social structures were beginning
to fracture. In a society that had been hierarchical,
with fixed reference points, to many people such
changes seemed revolutionary. Contemporaries used
the phrase "the world turned upside down" to
convey the radical changes that they saw around
them. Military control and the use of sequestration
enabled some people of "lower rank" to gain access
to land and wealth previously held by members of the
landed gentry, thus producing a fundamental change
(though often only temporarily) in the structure of
local society.

This can be clearly seen in the changes that took
place on the Brooke estate in Madeley parish.
Sir Basil Brooke was the largest landowner in Madeley.
A known Catholic, he was eventually committed
to the Tower in 1643 when implicated in a Royalist
plot. By 1645, Parliament sequestrated Brooke's
estate. This had allowed some people of lesser social
standing the opportunity to seize his land and
businesses for their own use. For example, Henry
Bowdler and Thomas Scott, both captains in the
Parliamentary army, gained control of his ironworks.
Bowdler together with John Pallett also secured estate
lands and subsequently reduced tenants rents to the
benefit of themselves and their friends. Although men
such as Bowdler and Pallett were relatively wealthy,
other beneficiaries came from a cross-section of
society that included Thomas Smithiman a blacksmith,
Francis Gough and Thomas Cope both tailors and
Richard Aston a labourer. However, between 1649-
1650 after a protracted legal struggle with the
Sequestration Committee the Madeley men lost
their petition for the lease of the estate to Edward
Cludd of Orlton, a relative of the Brooke family.
On the death of Cludd the estate passed to John
Wildman, notorious for being a speculator in
sequestrated land.

*The north wall of Tong Church, showing musket and
cannon damage dating to the Civil War*

The challenge to authority also found a very physical
expression in the destruction of many churches.
The changes to churches that had been implemented
by Archbishop Laud in the 1630s were an obvious
target. According to Gough "when the Parliament
had gott the upper hand of the King, they made an
ordinance, that the Comunion Railes should bee
pulled downe in every place..." those at Myddle were
"taken downe, and the Chancell floore was made level,
and the Communion Table placed in the middle of itt."

Other churches were damaged because they posed
a military or strategic threat as garrisons or fortifications.
A letter from Shrewsbury dated December 1645
noted "The whole town of Ercall is burnt, ye Church
demolished, all the Churches round about it are
uncovered." Richard Symonds observed that the
windows of Tong church were "much broken".
Other churches including Oswestry, Bishop's Castle,
Loppington, Benthall and Shrawardine were severely
damaged or destroyed during fighting. The decline
in reverence for places of holy worship was not only
by Parliament. A petition from the parishioners of
Clun to Parliament in 1647 complained that:

"Whereas a great part of our Church and Steeple, which was covered with lead and furnished with four bells, were during these late Troubles, burnt by an Officer of the Kings party (lest it should be made a Garrison for the Parliament ...)"

The effect of the war upon the Church was not confined to material matters. Some local clergy took a more pro-active role in the conflict. John Arnway, rector of Hodnet and Ightfield supplied "eight Troopers for his Majesty's service", while on the other side Samuel Berkely, Vicar of Clungunford, found himself imprisoned for disloyalty by Lord Capel, who had acted on accusations by some local parishioners. Other clergy took the third option available to them and fled from their livings, leaving their duties unattended. The parish register of Wrockwardine notes: "The Register was discontinued for some yeares by Mr. Smyth's deserting ye place in ye heate of ye Civill wars."

Women in the war

In many respects the written history of the Civil War has been male dominated. Very few women were actually involved in the fighting and consequently have been perceived as playing little part in the proceedings. This no doubt has been compounded by the fact that most accounts have been written by men. Recent studies have looked to rectify this position but in many cases the problems confronting historians are similar to investigations into the lives of ordinary people. Much more is known about the aristocracy and gentry because they have left us with a greater amount of written evidence.

Women did play a part in the war, often in a direct way. Many wives of gentlemen away at war had to organise and maintain large fortified houses in adverse conditions. Such women had great responsibility not only on a domestic front, but also, as they became military commanders. At Dawley Manor the lady owner garrisoned and defended the building against Parliament for a number of months in 1645 before her troops abandoned it for High Ercall. Fisher, in his Annals of Shrewsbury School, refers to Lady Lister holding Rowton Castle for a fortnight against Parliamentary forces under the command of Mytton, her husband having been taken prisoner at Shrewsbury. One of the most famous examples of such women was Brilliana Harley who commanded the garrison of Brampton Bryan Castle with much valour in the summer of 1643.

At the Battle of Wem in 1643 where the Royalists suffered an ignominious defeat there is evidence

The remains of Brampton Bryan Castle on the Shropshire-Herefordshire border, destroyed during the wars.

Lady Brilliana Harley

B.1598 d.1643. The wife of Robert Harley a prominent member of the Long Parliament, Lady Brilliana is most notably remembered for her defence of Brampton Bryan Castle on the Shropshire–Herefordshire border in 1643. Left in charge during the absence of her husband, she held out for over six weeks during a Royalist siege. Following this she took more aggressive action according to Priam Davies, a captain present throughout the hostilities, who wrote:

> "...This noble lady, who commanded in chief, I may truly say with such a masculine bravery, both
> for religion, resolution, wisdom, and warlike policy, that her equal I never yet saw, commanded that
> a party of about forty should go and beat up their quarters in Knighton, a market town in Radnorshire,
> four miles off, where Colonel Lingen's troops, her late antagonist was quartered. This was so performed
> that we brought some prisoners, arms and horses without the loss of one man."

Brilliana's letters provide us with an insight into the minds of the Puritan gentry on the South Shropshire border, and the religious tensions present in the area before and during the war. In June 1643 she wrote of her servant Peter, who had been held captive by the Royalists in Ludlow Castle, "He was grievously used in Ludlow. Turkes could have used him no worse; a leftenant Colonel Marrow would come every day and kick him up and down, and they laid him in a dungeon upon foul straw."

Brilliana died in October 1643 with Brampton Bryan under further threat. Brampton Bryan Castle was eventually captured by the Royalists in 1644 and subsequently destroyed.

that some women were involved in hand to hand fighting. The women, according to Garbett, "particularly distinguished themselves" which gave occasion to the ditty:

The women of Wem, and a few musketeers
Beat the Lord Capel, and all his Cavaliers

Another story relates to the survival of John Morris of The Hurst, who narrowly escaped death when rescued by two women. Taken prisoner during the siege of Hopton Castle, Morris was released by two maidservant who upon seeing his plight took two spits and "boldly went up to the soldiers and threatened to run them through if they did not let him go". The soldiers apparently released Morris who quickly made his escape.

Some women's involvement in the Civil War led them into the more dangerous and clandestine pursuits of espionage. A letter from the Parliamentary Committee of Salop to William Brereton, dated December 1645 reported: "The Woman you sent to Worcester came thence upon Saturday last and ... we shall impart in this what she sayeth ... that she overheard a discourse between Sir Wm. Vaughan and another soldier on Saturday last at Bridgnorth to this effect. He was to pass over at Holt Bridge and to take some advantage against Tarvin, which he heard was neglected and very slenderly manned..."

Female spies operated on both sides, occasionally encountering each other. In December 1645, Brereton received a further report of a female spy, it was noted

"...When she was with Vaughan at Bridgnorth, a gentlewoman came to him, to which Major-General Mytton had made a pass. She had some private discourse with him; at the close whereof he said to her, "You have given me very good intelligence and you may herein do us a great service". To whom she answered, "You may assure yourself I will do my best, for in so doing I shall do myself good."

Colonel Francis Billingsley, a Royalist, was slain in St. Leonard's Churchyard, Bridgnorth during Parliament's assault on the town in 1646. His sword was presented to the church some years later.

Obviously women were often caught up as civilian bystanders as at Oswestry when several were killed and wounded before the town fell to Parliament. However, the actions of some women at the siege also gives an insight into the prevailing attitudes to females in the seventeenth century, that is they were the 'weaker sex' and should receive chivalrous treatment on occasions. It is not clear to what extent besieged garrisons and towns played upon such notions of chivalry by using women in order to obtain quarter for their lives. At the siege of Oswestry Castle in 1644, the Parliamentary army of Lord Denbigh commanded by Thomas Mytton had initially refused quarter and prepared to burn the castle. Mytton recorded the events that followed:

> "My Lord . . .on his way there met him a party of women of all sorts down on their knees, confounding him with their Welsh howlings, that he was fain to get an Interpreter, which was to beseech me to intreat my Lord before he blew up the Castle, they might go up and speak to their husbands, children, and the officers; which ... my Lord condescended to ... Then my Lord to avoid the effusion of blood yet offered them mercy, if they would accept of it."

Women also followed armies on the march. A contemporary observer noted of the King's army:

> "The heterogeneous army that left Shrewsbury had a ... strange following of not only noble ladies and devoted wives, but a widely different class of females".

The mobility of soldiers during the Civil War occasionally facilitated new, and sometimes illicit, relationships. The absence of one woman's husband due to the war was often another soldier's opportunity. This was not necessarily confined to soldiers far away from home, local men in nearby garrisons also had a chance to act upon long held desires, such as Nathaniel Owen with the wife of Richard Manning at Myddle.

Some relationships ended in marriage, like Barnaby Rice "a souldier at Bentall" and Susan Davies married in November 1645 at Much Wenlock. Many did not.

It is not surprising to find entries in parish records for the baptism of illegitimate children. The register of baptisms between 1644-5 for the garrison town of Wem include "David, the son of a drum major", "Mary, daughter of Captaine Finch", and also Brian, a son of "John Bynama, cannoneer of Wem garrison".

These could have been the result of a happy union, but the alternative should not be discounted. Some women were victims of rape and sexual abuse. Little evidence of this comes to light because within the context of the period women would be unlikely to broadcast their ordeal, while their attackers were equally reluctant to announce their guilt. In some isolated rural areas there would be few witnesses. Accounts of ill treatment do exist, though the extent of violence is not always clear. Amongst the horrors of Hopton Castle where the men of the garrison were "butchered", two maids were also said to have been "roughly handled." Bearing in mind that the attackers had just stripped the garrison naked and beaten them to death one is left to ponder what the commentator's euphemism "roughly handled" really meant.

The harrowing effect upon individuals who witnessed violence cannot be underestimated. As a child, Richard Baxter's wife Margaret was present at the fall of Apley Castle:

> "It was stormed while she was in it, and part of the housing about it burnt, and men lay killed before her face, and all of them threatened and stripped of their clothing, so that they were fain to borrow clothes".

Margaret Baxter never completely recovered from this trial. A biographer noted that "A modern psychologist cannot fail to see in her gaiety an attempt to flee from reality, to suppress the memory of the storming of Apley Castle and to silence an awakening conscience."

The Civil War in Shropshire clearly affected the civilian population and when the war grew more intense as it drew to a close, ordinary people must have longed for peace and a return to normal life.

Gazeteer
Significant Shropshire Locations in the Civil War

Albright Hussey

The house at Albright Hussey, north of Shrewsbury, is reputed to have been built around 1524 and was originally owned by the Huse family. A carved panel displays the inscription "made by me Edward Huse, 1604". By the time of the Civil War, the house had become the property of Sir Pelham Corbet of Leigh, near Wem. During the war it was garrisoned by the Royalists as an outpost to Shrewsbury, countering the threat of Parliamentary forces situated in Wem. In 1644 a Parliamentary force attempted to take the garrison. Despite being out-numbered (they had only eight men and one sergeant), the garrison managed to thwart Parliament's ambitions by a cunning piece of deception, creating the illusion that the manor house was well defended. However, it was the action of one William Preece, known as "Scoggan", which finally drove their attackers away. He recognised one of the Parliamentary soldiers, a tailor from Hadnall called Bunny, whom he shot from a window with a fowling-piece. Bunny was injured in the leg and his horse was killed, his colleagues turned and fled.

Following this incident the garrison, according to Gough, was "soon after recalled at the request of Sir Pelham Corbet, he being apprehensive the soldiers would return and destroy his buildings".

Today the Albright Hussey is a restaurant. Scoggan's window can still be seen.

Apley Castle

Among the estates of the Charlton family was Apley Castle, near Wellington. Alan de Charleton fortified this mansion during the reign of Edward II. At the outbreak of the Civil War, Apley Castle was occupied by Thomas Hanmer and his wife, the widow of Francis Charlton.

Apley was not garrisoned until late 1643, after which Thomas Hanmer complained to Lord Capel about the activities of a local commander,

Lieutenant Hover, whose "exactions and plundering greatly annoyed the Country". However, Hanmer was arrested for high treason and the incident was only resolved when the Royalists, under the command of Prince Rupert, offered the beleaguered Mr Hanmer three choices, namely, "to maintain Appley Castle himself att his own charge, or leave it to another; or have it blowne up". Hanmer naturally chose the first.

Apley Castle was soon under threat from the Parliamentary forces of Wem, who were encouraged to take Apley by one of their supporters, Robert Charlton, the brother-in-law of Mrs Hanmer. Charlton had a hidden agenda, that is, he sought to become the legal guardian to the son and heir to Francis Charlton and control the Apley estate. In March 1644 Apley was taken by an army from Wem, but lost again to the Royalists under Sir William Vaughan when over two hundred soldiers were killed or taken prisoner. To prevent it falling into enemy hands again the Royalists destroyed the castle.

Apley House (Park)

Located near Bridgnorth and on the River Severn, Apley House was the seat of the Whitmore family. Sir William Whitmore erected it in 1572 possibly on the site of an earlier mansion. Whitmore had used money earned in London and can be seen as an example of new wealth being invested in land in Shropshire. His son, also named William, was an MP for Bridgnorth who supported the King. Little is known of the house as a Royalist garrison. However, shortly before the fall of Shrewsbury in 1645, Sir John Price, Governor of Montgomery for Parliament, became aware of a meeting at the house between some notable Royalists. Price was able to surround the house and capture the owner and his guests, which included "Sir William Whitmore, and Sir Thomas, his son, Sir Francis Ottley, Mr. Owen, Mr. Fowler, Mr. Griffiths, and divers other gentlemen of quality, and about sixty common Souldiers".

On hearing the news, Sir Michael Ernley issued an order to Sir John Kirk, Governor of Bridgnorth, to burn the house down as Parliament had failed to garrison it themselves. Sir John Weld (the Younger) representing the Whitmore family attempted to mediate on their behalf. However, events overtook them as Shrewsbury, including Weld, fell to Parliament. Sir William Whitmore's estate was sequestrated for payment of £583 3s. 2d. Much of the house still remains today.

Atcham

The bridge over the River Severn at Atcham was of obvious military importance, commanding both the river and one of the main routes into the town of Shrewsbury. It was, therefore, garrisoned in 1642 by the Royalists as an outpost of Shrewsbury. Soldiers were quartered in the church near to the old bridge (a new bridge was erected in the eighteenth century).

In 1644 Colonel Mytton attempted a daring raid on Atcham Bridge, wheeling around the town from Montford Bridge via Meole Brace. He disturbed various animals held there, including many horses, before retreating hastily from some advancing Royalist troops. The Royalists probably abandoned Atcham after the fall of Shrewsbury.

Benthall House

Built in 1535, near Broseley, this was the seat of the Benthall family. It was not occupied by any army until the Royalists garrisoned it in 1645. During the Civil War Laurence Benthall was made a Commissioner to raise money for Prince Rupert, but he was taken prisoner by Parliamentary forces during the fall of Shrewsbury and the house was subsequently abandoned by the Royalists and garrisoned by Parliament. Benthall was of strategic significance as it enabled the soldiers to disrupt the flow of goods and communications up and down the River Severn. It was also located in an area important for its coal production. Benthall remained in the hands of Parliament until the end of hostilities and Laurence Benthall's estate was sequestrated for £290.

Bishop's Castle

At the outbreak of war Bishop's Castle was divided. Of the two MPs that the borough returned to the House of Commons, Sir Robert Howard was a fervent Royalist while Richard More was a strong supporter of Parliament. The town made early preparations for war. In December 1642 the inhabitants were ordered to "keep the King's watch during the night ... [and] ... provide themselves

Atcham: An important crossing point over the River Severn and an outpost for the Royalist garrison in Shrewsbury.

Benthall House: Much prized by both sides in the later part of the Civil War for its proximity to the Severn and local minerals.

with a good and sufficient weapon." However, the townsfolk were not generally affected by the war until they were drawn into the hostilities towards the end of the conflict. A large body of men and women, known as Clubmen, fought to defend their property from both sides and maintain neutrality. They were especially active in Bishop's Castle. Their main grievances were towards the activities of soldiers from local Royalist garrisons under the command of the mercenary Vangeris, and the Royalists began to view Bishop's Castle as nominally for Parliament. On August 25th 1645, the main Royalist garrisons at Ludlow and Bridgnorth hoped to gather food and other goods by raiding a fair being held in Bishop's Castle. Four hundred horse and dragoons were sent to carry out the plan, but Parliament had been warned of the advance and dispatched eighty horse and eighty foot to meet them. A violent skirmish took place about a mile outside the town where the Royalists were badly defeated with "several" killed and two hundred taken prisoner. Because some of the local inhabitants had co-operated with Parliament, the notorious Royalist Sir William Vaughan razed part of the town in revenge and damaged the church because it had been used by Parliamentary soldiers and "for the preaching of sedition".

Boscobel House and White Ladies

In the east of the county close to the Staffordshire border lies Boscobel House, a hunting lodge erected by John Giffard c.1630. It was a friend, Sir Basil Brook of Madeley, who supposedly named the house "Boscobel" from the Italian phrase *Bosco Bello* meaning beautiful or fair woods. By the outbreak of war the house had passed to Frances Cotton, daughter of John Giffard. The Giffards were Catholics and the family's religion caused them to side with the King. However, it was the part that Boscobel played during the flight of Charles II, where the King hid up an Oak tree after fleeing the battle of Worcester in 1651, that has reserved its place in history.

The Giffard family also owned neighbouring White Ladies, a house built in the grounds of the old twelfth century Augustinian priory. It was to White ladies that Charles first fled on 4th September 1651 before returning to Boscobel after an abortive attempt to cross the River Severn at Madeley. White Ladies was demolished during the eighteenth century and only some remains of the priory survive.

Boscobel House and the "Royal Oak" have been preserved by English Heritage. It provides an excellent example of a Jacobean hunting lodge. The interior, most notably the priest holes, also highlights the lifestyle of a Catholic household.

Bridgnorth

The ancient town of Bridgnorth had a population of about two thousand two hundred in the 1630's. The town had benefited from the increase in river trade in the seventeenth century, especially through the carrying of coal both into and out of the county. Malt was another common commodity. The river trade was so important that in a resolution dated 1635 the Bridgnorth Corporation opposed the improvement of the Warwickshire Avon arguing:

"That it will be very great damage to this country in carryinge away coles and other

fuel and butter and cheese, which is the life and chiefe supportation of the same, and it will hinder bringing up of the Low Country malt into this Country, and will cause corn to be dearer in our markets, hinder the common commerce and traffic which wee have with other Countrys, and be divers other ways very prejudicial to this Country".

Bridgnorth, therefore, held an important strategic position along the River Severn. It was also located on the road between Shrewsbury, Worcester and the Midlands. The Royalists made an early attempt to secure it for the King. In 1642 Prince Rupert called upon the Jury of Bridgnorth to choose "of such men for your Bayliffes as yee are sure are well affected for his Majesty's Service." Although there were some opponents in the town, it was sufficiently safe

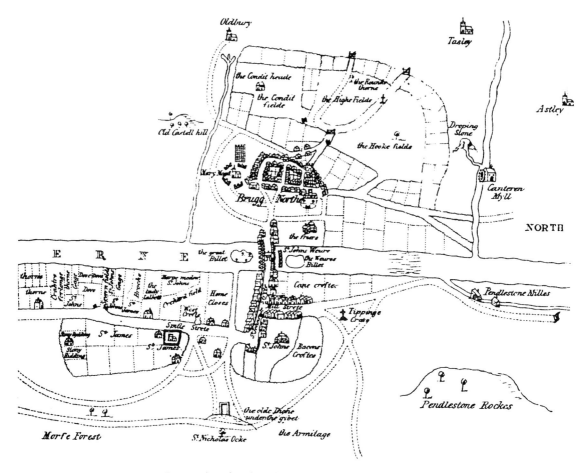

From a plan of Bridgnorth in the early seventeenth century.

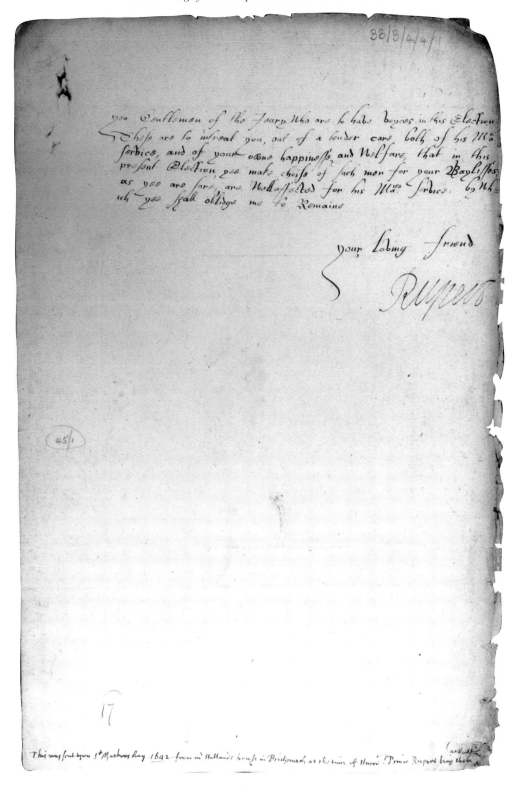

A letter from Prince Rupert to the Bridgnorth Jury, demanding the town's support for the King

Bridgnorth Castle had a commanding view over the Severn Valley, but was destroyed during Parliament's final assault on the town in 1646.

for the king to visit it when he moved to and from Shrewsbury, in October 1642. In April 1643 fortifications were increased "at all fords, and places about this towne" and it became a secure Royalist garrison. Charles visited the town again in July 1645 when circling the Midlands after his defeat at Naseby, and also the following September after an abortive attempt to relieve Chester.

Many rumours surround the town's involvement in the war, notably the visit of Oliver Cromwell. He never visited the town though some chroniclers relate a story describing him being shot at. This is a confusion of places with the writers probably mistaking Bridgewater for Bridgnorth. Similarly an account of a skirmish between Essex and Rupert early in the war is probably untrue.

When Bridgnorth did see action it was certainly dramatic. In 1645 the Shrewsbury garrison were able to take a hundred and eighty horses and some prisoners in a surprise raid. They drove the Royalist troops into the castle which they were unable to secure.

However in 1646 the town and castle finally fell to Parliament with severe damage being inflicted on the town by fire. The castle was blown up and some small remains of it can be seen today.

Broncroft Castle

According to Leland in c.1540 Broncroft Castle was "a very goodly place like a Castle, belonging to the Earl of Shrewsbury, and standith on Clee Hill". During the Civil War it was owned by the Lutley family and was garrisoned for the King.

In June 1645, the retreating Royalists abandoned the garrison and attempted to destroy it. Parliament was aware of its importance as a gateway to Ludlow and, according to contemporary sources, they "fell to repair and fortifie it".

On July 4th 1645 Royalist forces led by Sir William Vaughan, attacked the garrison and parliamentary troops under the command of Captain Ashton who were stationed in the vicinity. The Royalists, numbering three to four hundred men, heavily defeated the opposing forces. Mercurius Aulicus reported that Vaughan's army "killed many of them in the place, and took prisoners Captaine Ashton, a Coronet, and 47 Troopers, with their armes, and 80 good horses."

Despite this setback, the garrison maintained its activities. In the following January Sir Thomas Edwardes complained to fellow Royalist Sir Francis Ottley "I lately suffered from Bromcroft Castle, the Lord deliver us out of the hands of these oppressors".

Parliament later abandoned and destroyed the castle. Broncroft was restored in the nineteenth century and one of the original towers has survived.

Buildwas

Located on the River Severn, Buildwas was of some importance to both sides. Here, a bridge (demolished in 1690) formed a vital link across the Severn while also enabling those who commanded it to exert control over river traffic. Nearby were crucial supplies of ordnance from foundries at Leighton, Madeley and Coalbrookdale. Little is known of the garrison that was placed at Buildwas during the Civil War. At the outbreak of hostilities, James Lacon of West Coppice was ordered to employ some men to build a spiked turnstile on the bridge to block the passage of horse. At some point in the conflict both sides held it.

Caus Castle

West of Shrewsbury, near the Welsh border, is the ancient manor of Caus, first granted to Roger Corbet by William I. Archaeological evidence suggests that there was once a sizeable settlement below the castle. A charter to hold a market was granted by King John. During the reign of Edward III it was owned by the Earls of Stafford, and in the sixteenth century by Robert Howard. At the beginning of the Civil War the Castle was owned by Sir Henry Thynne, a Royalist landowner who exerted considerable pressure upon some of his tenants to fight for the King.

By 1645 the Florentine mercenary Captain Davallier was in command of an imposing garrison at Caus. Located on a steep ridge between two valleys encompassed by a ditch and a wall, the castle was virtually impregnable.

The 'Kingdomes Weekly Intelligence' reported that it was "a place of great strength ... it standing on a rock not mineable."

In June 1645 Parliamentary forces sieged the castle, which now contained three hundred men, for seven days until it surrendered. Parliament's Mercurius Veredicus joyfully announced that "The Governor refusing to deliver it upon summons, our forces began to storm it for a while; at length the enemy put forth a white flag."

Following its surrender the castle was destroyed. Its owner, Sir Henry Thynne was later imprisoned in Shrewsbury and afterwards in the Fleet. His estates were sequestrated for £1,760, with £200 to be settled "on a church". The remains of the castle can still be seen today.

Clun

The castle at Clun had fallen into ruin before the Civil War. This made Clun less important as a military centre than other neighbouring towns and villages during hostilities.

The lord of the manor, Sir Robert Howard, signed the "Declaration of the Shropshire gentry" in support of the King. He was instrumental in raising forces for the Royalist cause and commanded a regiment of dragoons. Clun was held for the Royalists for a significant part of the war, despite many prominent Puritans in and around the town. It was involved directly in the war in 1644 when Royalist soldiers were billeted in the church.

The soldiers had either been sent to deal with the Clubmen, or soldiers of the hated mercenary Vangeris. Whoever commanded them, they were responsible for burning the church.

The Royalists further antagonised the local population when Prince Maurice held Thomas Brome, the warden of Holy Trinity Hospital almshouses, to ransom in order to raise money or the war effort. They also damaged part of the building.

Coalbrookdale

Site of an ironworks owned by Basil Brooke. The original furnace dated 1638 with the initials BB can still be seen. It was used for supplying ordnance during the war. As a supporter of the King, Brooke lost the furnace, among other estates, to Parliamentarians. The Darby family enlarged the furnace in the eighteenth century and today the restored remains are open to the public next to the Museum of Iron.

Condover Hall

Condover estate was acquired by the Owen family in the sixteenth century. The house was erected by Sir Roger Owen, an MP and High Sheriff of Shropshire in 1604, the son of Thomas Owen a notable Judge. It eventually passed to his brother Sir William Owen, also High Sheriff in 1623. There is much controversy surrounding the political allegiance of Sir William Owen. He was made a Commissioner of Array by the King but was widely believed to be in close correspondence with the Parliamentary Committee at Wem. Indeed, charges of "treachery" were made against Owen and other "professed" Royalists who it was supposed aided the easy capture of Shrewsbury by the Parliamentarians. Condover Hall was apparently offered to Parliament as a garrison. This may explain why Owen received only a relatively small fine of £314, yet by 1656 Sir William Owen was imprisoned in Shrewsbury because of his antipathy to the Commonwealth government. It was only through an act of leniency by Colonel James Berry, Major General for Shropshire, that Owen was finally released.

Dawley Castle

Little is known of the history surrounding Dawley Castle. During the Civil War it seems to have been held as a Royalist garrison until the middle of 1645. Despite growing pressure from Parliamentary forces, who were reducing the few remaining Royalist garrisons in the County, it was held and maintained by its lady owner. The building was abandoned in August 1645 when the garrison fled to High Ercall.

Renewed Royalist efforts in the County during the second Civil War brought about plans to take Dawley Castle in 1648. Among the plotters were Sir Francis Ottley, Sir Henry Lingen and a Colonel Dudley who commanded some troops who had gathered in Boscobel Wood. However, the plan

was exposed by Captain Yarrington, formerly of the garrison at Madeley Church, who surprised some two hundred royalist troops. The Commons ordered the destruction of the castle. No remains of the Castle can be located today.

Dudleston SEE ELLESMERE

Eaton Constantine

The notable Puritan Richard Baxter grew up in this parish, near the Severn between Buildwas and Shrewsbury. His house is still standing today (see photo p. 9 and essay on Baxter, chapter 1).

Ellesmere

Troops of both sides moving along the borders of Cheshire and Wales, and between Oswestry and Whitchurch continually harassed the inhabitants of the small market town of Ellesmere. Several skirmishes also took place near the town. On 12th January 1644 Mytton surprised the Royalist Governor of Chester, Sir Nicholas Byron, who was transporting ammunition to that city from Shrewsbury. By this action Parliament secured itself eight large barrels of powder, 7cwt. of match, other ammunition and two hundred and fifty horses. Sir Nicholas Byron, Sir Richard Willis and his brother Major Willis, a hundred officers and men were taken prisoner.

Mytton was again active in the area on the 19th June the same year. Two prisoners had given information relating to a small convoy heading toward Bangor. Parliamentary troops led by Mytton attempted to surprise the party at Dudleston. The plan was successful despite the convoy numbering twice as many troops as had been expected.

More importantly, some of the captives informed Mytton that Oswestry had a mere sixty foot left to hold the Royalist garrison. This encouraged Parliament to make their final assault on that town.

High Ercall House

Built in 1608, High Ercall House was the seat of the Newport family. The building was fortified for the King around Easter 1644. As soon as they had taken Shrewsbury, Parliamentary forces turned their attention towards the garrison of High Ercall. In April 1645 the Weekly Account optimistically reported:

"Lieutenant Colonel Reinking with a party
of Shropshire forces ... came before the
enemy's Garrison of High Arkall ...
they have shot away 20 barrels of powder ...
[and] ... they have slaine and wounded
many; beate down the drawbridge, and made
a great breach into the Church".

Led by Sir Vincent Corbet, the garrison fought
off their attackers and five hundred Parliamentary
soldiers were either killed, wounded or taken
prisoner. The siege was abandoned on 14th April.
By July, High Ercall was besieged again and
surrounded by 1,100 Parliament horse and foot.
This time Royalists forces killed a hundred men
and took around three hundred and fifty prisoners,
amongst whom was the mercenary Reinking.
Other soldiers were apparently drowned during
their retreat from the battlefield.

Together with Ludlow and Bridgnorth,
High Ercall represented the only Royalist garrisons
left in Shropshire by the end of 1645.
However, Parliament could not easily breach the
strong defences. A contemporary Parliamentarian
source noted that High Ercall was "a strong place
and well fortified, and having a deep moat about it,
and in regard of the situation of it, not thought
feasible to be taken by storm". In March 1646
Parliament besieged the house again. An attempt
at its relief by Sir Jacob Astley and the Governor
of the Garrison, who had been absent at the
beginning of the siege, was repelled. On the 28th
March, the garrison finally surrendered. The house
was not destroyed, The Committee of Both
Kingdoms deciding that the sieges had left "too
many sad marks ... of the calamity of this war."

Holgate Castle

The Helget family erected Holgate Castle in
Corvedale during the Norman period. By the
outbreak of war it was owned by the Cressett
family. From the little evidence that is available
it would appear that the Royalists garrisoned the
castle, using it as an outpost for Ludlow. After the
fall of Shrewsbury in 1645, with Parliament
thrusting southwards, the Royalists quit the
garrison and destroyed the castle. In the June of
that year Parliamentary forces en route to Ludlow
had recorded two castles in Corvedale, that is
Holgate and Broncroft. They chose to rebuild and

fortify the latter, and left Holgate to stand in ruin.
The site of the keep and moat can be identified
today, while part of an old tower still remains.

Hopton Castle

Originally owned by the Hopton family, by the
1640s it was held by Henry Wallop a supporter
of Parliament. In February 1644, it was fortified
as an outpost of Brampton Bryan Castle.
Lieutenant Wright, a doctor who maintained
Brampton Bryan after the death of Lady Brilliana
Harley, gained intelligence of Royalist intentions
to fortify and strengthen a small garrison at
Hopton Castle. In response he ordered twenty
soldiers from Brampton Bryan to seize the castle,
which they accomplished without loss.
The Royalists under Sir Michael Woodhouse laid
siege to the castle. The Commander of the
garrison, Samuel More, carefully logged the details
of the events that followed.

Beginning on the 18th February, the Royalists
had apparently made several unsuccessful attempts
to storm the castle resulting in the deaths of many
soldiers, despite the garrison containing only
31 men. A week later they returned with a cannon
and other pieces of ordinance, but still the
defenders refused to capitulate and killed another
150 soldiers. Finally, the Royalists decided to mine
and set fire to the castle with the intention of
blowing it up. At this point the garrison decided
to surrender in return for their lives.
Although Colonel Woodhouse refused to give
a guarantee of safety, More recalled that "we all
thought we should only be made prisoners, and did
not think of such a death as hereafter appears ...
About three hours after the delivery of the Castle,
Lieut. Aldersea asked me how many soldiers were
sent to Shrewsbury? I said all. Then he told me
none: all were killed." The siege had cost the lives
of over two hundred Royalist soldiers and a severe
act of retribution was embarked upon, ending in
the cold-blooded massacre of 29 prisoners.
In a letter to the sister of one of the dead,
Major Phillips, More wrote:

"He (Phillips) as all the rest, was unmercifully
killed. Your brother offered £20 to save his
life. They took him and brought him into the
Castle to receive the money ... They swore
at him and stabbed him. Presently all the rest,

being 28 in number, were killed with clubs and such things after they were stripped naked. Two maids they stripped and cut, but some helped them to escape."

For the Royalists, the taking of Hopton Castle was the cause for celebration. Ludlow Churchwardens Accounts note: "for drinke to ye Ringers at the taking of Hopton Castle ... 1s. 6d." To prevent it from being used as a garrison in the future, the castle was dismantled but its ruins still stand today.

Langley Chapel

Langley Chapel is a stark and austere building, situated in the middle of a field near Acton Burnell. It is interesting as an example of an Elizabethan church, the only new one to be built in Shropshire during her reign. Devoid of any decoration or icons, it reflects the obsessive anti-Catholic nature of the reformation. It is not a Puritan church but simply one that reflected the fashion of the late sixteenth century. The church interior predates the Laudian reforms of the 1630s that were to signal a return to more traditional and ritualistic symbols of hierarchy, such as altar rails and raised pulpits. It is interesting to compare it with other Shropshire churches that had been built earlier when Catholicism was still the established religion.

Lea Hall (Castle)

Little is known about this 14th century castle. Its remains adjoin a 19th century farmhouse. The castle was certainly garrisoned by Royalists who held Bishop's Castle about a mile and a half to the west, though there is no record of when this took place. The local population had found the garrison such a nuisance that the Clubmen demanded its removal. However, on October 18th 1645, it was recorded that:

"Sir Thomas Middleton hath performed much gallant service: and in particular he sent forth a party of foot to Leigh (Lea) about a mile from Bishop's Castle, where the enemy had left a garrison, which fled away before his forces came neare them."

The castle was later abandoned and no doubt destroyed by Parliamentary forces.

Leigh Hall (Worthen)

At the outbreak of war, the Corbet family owned Leigh Hall. The fortified house was probably on the site of the old fourteenth century manor of the Corbets of Leigh-Juxta-Caus. The Royalists occupied it as a garrison and installed the mercenary Davallier as governor. This Florentine soldier also controlled Caus Castle and used both to exact money and supplies from the inhabitants to the west and the south of the county. In 1646, the house was abandoned by the Royalists and burnt down. Some remains can still be seen today, in particular a moat, some fragments of a wall and foundations of a gatehouse.

Lilleshall

Lilleshall Abbey was fortified by its owner, Sir Richard Leveson a Royalist. It was garrisoned by Captain Bostock and a hundred and sixty soldiers, who on the 25th March 1644 joined forces with troops from Wellington under the command of Vaughan and Ellis who proceeded to defeat Mytton in an open battle near Longford. Eventually Major Braine captured the Abbey for Parliament in 1645. The Governor was killed during the fighting. The garrison was allowed to march away without their weapons.

Longford House

This property, near Newport, belonged to the Earl of Shrewsbury. Richard Symonds called it "a large brick house and seate, spoiled and abused." It was garrisoned by Parliament and Richard Baxter served as chaplain for several weeks until he secured the release of his father, who had been taken hostage by Royalist troops from Lilleshall Abbey. In a battle near the house, a Parliamentary army under Mytton was defeated by Vaughan and Ellis, losing two hundred men, about one-third of their forces. In April 1644 the Royalists commanded by Sergeant Major Skrimshaw captured the house. The garrison of one hundred musketeers under a Captain Parry was allowed to march away without their weapons. However, many subsequently went over to the Royalist forces under Prince Rupert. The King's nephew most probably destroyed much of the house.

Longner

This house was the seat of the Burton family. They had been at Longner since the early fifteenth century. It was garrisoned by the Royalists because of its strategic location on the River Severn, near Atcham. The owner at the time, Francis Burton, appeared to be a supporter of the King, although he seemed keen to remove the soldiers from the house in order to preserve it. He therefore agreed to "maintain 8 musketeers" for the Royalists and the rest of the garrison was sent to defend Montford Bridge. It is interesting that Francis Burton supported the King as his descendants had Puritan leanings. Furthermore, his son and heir, Thomas Burton, sat on the Commission that tried Captain Benbow for changing sides and supporting Charles II in 1651, and associated with local Presbyterians.

The garrison was eventually abandoned after the fall of Shrewsbury in 1645. The house itself was knocked down and rebuilt in the eighteenth century.

Loppington

This was the scene of a dramatic skirmish in 1643 when the Royalists attacked some Parliamentary dragoons in Loppington. They were driven into the church where the roof and porch were set on fire and were forced to surrender. However, they were not prisoners for long. Having heard the disturbance, a force of two hundred foot soldiers and three hundred cavalry from Wem rescued them and drove the Royalists back towards their base at Prees Heath.

Ludlow

The old market town of Ludlow stands on the confluence of the Corve and the Teme in the south of the county. By the seventeenth century it had developed a diverse and varied economy. Although the town lost some income as a result of the Shrewsbury drapers' monopoly of the woollen trade, other trades thrived. Between 1614-1667 over two hundred different occupations were known to exist within the town, including ironmongers, cutlers, weavers, fullers, tanners, glovers, apothecaries, barbers and booksellers. Its population in 1641 was 2,600. Like other towns, however, it was susceptible to plague. In the autumn of 1609, about a hundred and twenty-seven people were killed. It also reached high levels in the town between 1623-1624 and in 1636.

The Council of the Marches sat at Ludlow and governed Wales, Worcester, Herefordshire and Shropshire. Staffed by professional lawyers and local

dignitaries, it was effectively a Royal court and regional government hearing cases as diverse as adultery and incest to fraud and forgery. In 1621 the Council ordered bailiffs to put William Webbe in the pillory for forgery and bribery. Much of the work, however, was mundane. On the 4th September 1634, the Court arbitrated between William Barrett, George Illedge and others, concerning the right to a "pew or kneeling place in the North side of the parish church of Alberbury next to the pulpit and above the seat of Thomas Rider".

The Council's work provided Ludlow with a large income, bringing business and jobs to the town. Between 1615-1616 the court paid 10s. to William Pringle who cleaned the Castle walls, while Francis Bosley received 18s. for bringing linen from London. This was in addition to all the services, such as accommodation, provided to attorneys, clerks and others who carried out business in the Court. The decision by the Long Parliament to dismantle this Royal court in 1641 was very unpopular both within the town and throughout the surrounding area and gave the local gentry an extra incentive to follow the Royalist cause, hardening their naturally conservative perspective.

Ludlow was of great strategic importance to both sides in the Civil War. The town stood on the route from Shrewsbury to Hereford and the west of England. Its castle provided an almost impregnable position for those who held it. Garrisoned by the Royalists, it briefly came under threat in May 1643 from Parliamentary forces to the south.
The inhabitants who lived outside the town were ordered to build a fence or rampart 45 inches high and 36 inches thick. Because of the strength of Ludlow, the Royalists were able to hold most of south Shropshire throughout the war. Prince Rupert used it as a base when recruiting in Wales and Herefordshire. The King also visited the town after his defeat at Naseby in the summer of 1645.

The town finally came under direct attack as Parliament increased its grip on the county in 1646. In April of that year Colonel John Birch besieged the town with over a thousand troops. The defending garrison of roughly three hundred and fifty were forced back behind the town walls having set fire to some but not all of the houses outside. Both sides then settled down to a war of attrition for five weeks as the Parliamentary forces prepared their positions and artillery with which to bombard the defenders before a final attack. In May 1646 a Parliamentary commentator wrote that:

> "absolute agreement was made for the surrender of Ludlow to the Parliament, to be June the first. The officers to march away with horses and armes, and the men without. What was in the Castle we'll tell you when we have it."

The Governor of Ludlow, Sir Michael Woodhouse, initially reneged on the deal, refusing to surrender to anyone but Colonel Birch. Woodhouse feared retribution from Shropshire troops because he was in command at the massacre of the garrison at Hopton Castle. He was prepared to fight on rather than give himself up to these soldiers "whereupon Colonel Birch was sent for, being come, they resigned unto him without further dispute."

After the fall of Ludlow to Parliament there were few incidents of note. Much effort concentrated upon the repair of the considerable physical damage to buildings that had been inflicted upon the town. Parliament ordered that Shrewsbury and Ludlow alone in the county should have military garrisons. In 1648 a Royalist plot was discovered to surprise Ludlow Castle but was easily thwarted by the authorities. The garrison at Ludlow was disbanded in 1655.

Lydbury North

The church at Lydbury North, near Bishop's Castle, contains two large candlestick holders dating from 1630s which are surviving examples of the symbolic and ritualistic reforms of Archbishop Laud.

Madeley and Madeley Court

Basil Brooke, head of one of the most important Catholic families in the county, owned Madeley Court. Before the outbreak of the Civil War,

Madeley Court, the former home of Basil Brooke, an influential Catholic and supporter of the King. Now used as an hotel.

some Puritans believed that Brooke was involved in a Catholic plot. Although such rumours were probably based upon hearsay, many viewed his activities at Madeley Court with suspicion. During the war Madeley Court was garrisoned for the King, as was Madeley Church. Both appear to have been abandoned in 1646. Parliament sequestrated Brooke's estate as punishment for siding with the King, but much of the estate returned to the family some years later. The largely Jacobean exterior of Madeley Court and its gatehouse can still be seen today. The building is now a hotel.

At Madeley, Charles II hid in a barn while fleeing from Parliament after the battle of Worcester in 1651. He was attempting to cross the River Severn at a nearby ford. Today a plaque reveals the hiding place of the King.

Majors Leap (SEE WILDERHOPE)

Market Drayton

Market Drayton was a relatively prosperous market town in a rich dairy region.

At the beginning of war it was occupied by Parliamentary forces under the command of Sir William Brereton. Vincent Corbet attempted its capture for the King in April 1643, but his army was driven out by Parliamentary forces from Nantwich before it could be fortified. Thomas Malbon records in his diary: "Nantwich forces did noe wronge nor harm to the Towne, but only threw down their workes, after the Cavaliers were all fled and slain and taken prisoners."

The Royalists made a further attempt to secure the town in the following September, without success. In March 1644 Market Drayton was attacked by Prince Rupert, who hoped to engage Sir Thomas Fairfax and the Earl of Denbigh. Although the large Parliamentary force received intelligence of Rupert's plan and were prepared for the onslaught, they were no match for Rupert's military skill and were forced to flee the town having lost twenty-two men and had forty captured.

The King stayed in the vicinity of the town on his way north in 1645, but hearing news of the siege of Oxford was forced to return south.

Montford Bridge

West of Shrewsbury on the River Severn, Montford Bridge was a strategic crossing. The town's Corporation fortified it as an outpost of Shrewsbury in 1642. It was the scene of a skirmish on the 3rd of May 1644 when one hundred new Royalist recruits en route to Shrewsbury were captured by Parliamentary cavalry. Parliamentary forces under Denbigh captured the bridge itself in July the same year. His troops went on to Shrewsbury, but were not strong enough to attempt a real attack and, falling back across the Severn to rejoin their forces at Wem, they burned the bridge.

Moreton Corbet Castle

"Upon the river Roden" wrote Camden "Moreton Corbet, anciently a house of the Turret family, afterwards a castle of the Corbets showed itself, where, within our memory, Robert Corbet, to gratify his taste for architecture, began in a barren place a most grand and stately building after the Italian model. But death preventing his designs carried him off, so that he left the new work unfinished and the old Castle defaced. He was sheriff of Shropshire in 1573, and died in 1578."

At the outbreak of war, Sir Vincent Corbet, a fervent Royalist owned the castle, but it was not garrisoned for the King until late 1643. In 1644 it was attacked by Reinking who, pretending that his forces were much bigger than they were, succeeded in capturing it.

Moreton Corbet remained in the hands of Parliament until the fall of Shrewsbury when it was destroyed. Its remains still stand.

Myddle

In 1701 Richard Gough, from the village of Myddle, completed a history of the parish. This detailed account is remarkable as a source for historians as it gives a complete picture of a rural community during the seventeenth century. Gough was a young boy at the outbreak of the war but remembered various incidents and stories which he recounts in an entertaining style, giving us not only anecdotal factual details but an insight into the seventeenth century mind and the concerns and beliefs of his period.

The fact that Myddle was a typical village makes this an important snapshot, giving us a feel for the impact the war had on many quiet small communities throughout England.

Many buildings still remain from the period and can be clearly identified from the text.

Newport

Newport is situated on the border with Staffordshire in the east of the county and stood on the main road from London to Chester which was then the main port connecting England to Ireland. The King passed through the town on his way to Shrewsbury in 1642. It was effectively Royalist throughout the war, but dominated by the garrisons around it which increasingly fell to Parliament. In December 1644, the townspeople refused to give their weekly payment to the Royalist Governor of Shrewsbury. Like other places, their loyalty swung from one side to another depending on military and economic pressures.

Skirmishes around these garrisons inevitably spilled into the outskirts of the town. In 1644, fighting near Longford (qv), where the Royalists defeated a Parliamentary force under Mytton, seems to have spread along the Strine brook. Some archaeological evidence, including several human remains, appear to confirm this. In May 1645 Charles again passed through the town en route for Chester, William Brereton noted:

> "The King's army hath continued ever since Saturday night within sixteen miles of Nantwich, the King himself at Mr Piggott's of Chetwynd, the two Princes at the Swan in Newport, their whole army thereabouts."

The "Princes" were Rupert and Maurice. Their regiments, camped in the vicinity of the town, were continually harried by Parliament soldiers from Staffordshire. A regiment of horse under Captain Stone "fell upon some of them that night in their quarters, took sixty horse, many men in arms and slew twenty in the fight".

Newport also saw fighting after the first Civil War. Following the Battle of Worcester in 1651, Charles II escaped towards Boscobel. His bodyguard detached themselves and headed north, but at Newport they were confronted by

Parliament and battle ensued. During the fighting, one of the King's men, Lord Talbot, escaped to Longford Hall. Meanwhile, the Duke of Buckingham, along with Colonel Blague, fled towards Forton where they were attacked by Colonels Lilburne and Blundel. They managed to escape to Bloore Park near Cheswardine. Buckingham, like Charles II, eventually found his way to France and safety.

Oswestry

Oswestry saw a good deal of fighting in the war. Being a walled town in the Marches with its own castle, it was a significant prize for either side to hold. It was garrisoned by the Royalists in 1643 and several buildings outside the walls were destroyed in order to protect the town's defences. The church steeple was demolished so the enemy could not fire or observe from it. The Governor was Edward Lloyd of Llanforda, who was nearly captured by Mytton after accepting a dinner invitation from his enemy. As a result he was replaced by Sir Absetts Shipman, who was absent when Oswestry was attacked by Mytton and Denbigh in June 1644. The Royalists had been right to see the church as a threat as Mytton placed his cannon on the ruined building and was therefore able to dominate the town. Having bombarded the new gate the Parliamentarians stormed the town forcing the garrison into the castle.

An anecdote relayed by local historians recounts the story that "a bold youth named George Cranage went with his hatchet, and let down the chains of the drawbridge, over which the horsemen passed immediately". The Royalists retreated into the Castle, and the inhabitants also fled for shelter. Cranage was then persuaded to fasten a petard or small bomb to the Castle Gate. "Being enlivened with wine", he crept from one house to another, until he drew near the Castle. He "sprang to the Gate ... set fire to it, and escaped unhurt". The explosion burst open the Castle Gate causing the garrison to offer their surrender. The surrender was remarkably negotiated by some of the local women who managed to secure quarter for the lives of the soldiers. To avoid plunder, the town's Corporation agreed to surrender £500 as compensation. Lord Denbigh installed Mytton as Governor.

The Royalists quickly made plans to recapture Oswestry. Sir Fulke Hunckes, Governor of

Shrewsbury, raised a force of around fifteen hundred horse and three and a half thousand foot to take the town, but reinforced by Sir Thomas Middleton, the garrison survived. Middleton wrote, "the enemy had taken the passage of water neer Whittington, and very furiously assaulted and charged us, but were repulsed" and they "beat back" the enemy "to a place called Felton Heath."

This gave Parliament its second major foothold in Shropshire. From this town and Wem, it was possible to establish some measure of control over North Shropshire.

Rowton Castle

The Lister family held Rowton Castle, west of Shrewsbury, for many years. The owner at the outbreak of war was Thomas Lister who made a gift of 500 guineas to the King in Shrewsbury for which he received a knighthood. Thomas Lister was later taken prisoner at Shrewsbury and it has been claimed that Rowton was maintained by Lady Lister, who defended the castle against Mytton in 1645. The castle was eventually surrendered by the Royalists and destroyed by Parliament in that same year. Rowton Castle has since been rebuilt. It is this relatively modern structure which can be seen today.

Shrawardine

Shrawardine was a medieval castle built by John Fitz Alan around 1250 on the site of a former fortification. Sir William Vaughan, "The Devil of Shrawardine", garrisoned it for the Royalists in September 1644. The church and much of the village were destroyed in an attempt to strengthen the defences and reduce cover for attackers. When Parliament's forces did besiege the castle, it only held out for five days. Vaughan was not present and this may account for the capitulation. The garrison was allowed to march away to Ludlow. Fearing that Vaughan would try to recapture it, the castle was destroyed, and the stones carried to Shrewsbury where they were used to repair its castle.

Shrewsbury

By the mid-1630s, the county town of Shrewsbury had a population of around six and a half thousand. By 1670 it was the fifteenth largest town in England outside London with a population of 7,100. In the sixteenth century the town was famous for its involvement with the woollen trade. The drapers of Shrewsbury held a monopoly over the trade of cloth from Wales and merchant families like the Rowleys, Lloyds, and Irelands built large houses in the town, some of which remain today. Thomas Jones, known as "the rich Jones", was reputed to be worth between £30,000 and £40,000 in 1638. Such wealth may account for the comparatively high assessment for Ship Money imposed on the town in the 1630s.

Shrewsbury had a growing number of shops and businesses which included traditional trades such as shoemakers and glovers and also new occupations - upholsterers, silk-weavers, booksellers, watchmakers, refiners, market gardeners, pipe makers and manufacturers of "aqua vitae". In 1612 a new pinfold was erected at Coleham for livestock, reflecting the increased trade in agricultural produce at the markets and fairs held both inside and outside the town. There were four fairs and by 1638 another two had been added.

The River Severn was the main transport link. Roads were extremely poor and navigable rivers provided the best means of transporting goods at this time. England's longest river and one of the most important transport arteries, was navigable from Pool Quay near Welshpool, to its estuary at Bristol. Barges and trows transported all manners of goods. Such was the volume of traffic that two new quays were built at Mardol and Frankwell in 1607 and 1608. Trows able to carry thirty tons of cargo carried downstream goods such as cheese, calfskins, bacon, butter, glue, tallow, timber, cereals and linen. On return they carried wine, sugar, spices, citrus fruit, raisins, and tobacco imported from overseas. Raw cotton would also be shipped upstream and distributed into the farms and cottages of Shropshire to be worked on and the finished cloth was later collected and shipped downstream.

Not everyone benefited, however. There is evidence of poverty in Shrewsbury throughout this period. Between 1642-3 one in six were in receipt of poor relief. In such small urban populations the effects of sporadic outbreaks of plague could also easily increase the numbers of those who needed

The King's retinue was accommodated in the Old Shrewsbury School (above), now a public library.

assistance. In December 1631 the people of Bridgnorth collected money "towards the relief of the poore of ye Towne of Shrewsbury, visited with ye Plague".

During the Civil War, Shrewsbury was looked upon by both sides as an important prize. As a walled town with a castle dating from medieval times, it provided a formidable defensive position to siege. The Royalists managed to organise first and claim the town. The corporation invited Charles to the town as he was marching westwards from Nottingham and the King entered the town on the 20th September and took up residence in the Council House. His entourage stayed in the nearby Shrewsbury School. Both buildings are still standing today.

The King did not stay long. He left on the 22nd to recruit troops in Chester and the Welsh borders, returned on the 27th and then stayed until the

12th October. During his stay a Royal Mint was established under the direction of Thomas Bushell of Aberystwyth. Using silver plate donated by the local populace he was thus able to pay his soldiers with newly coined money. The mint continued for a further year in the town. It is thought that the mint was situated in Bennett's mansion, though an alternative site may have been at Bellstone House. Charles also established a print works in Charlton Hall in the house of Basil Waring in order to print Royalist propaganda. The bulk of the army was camped at the Gay Meadow in Abbey Foregate until they moved south. An order, dated 12th October 1642, showed that some travelled by water. John Studley, The Mayor of Shrewsbury, requested "Three able and sufficient trowmen to carry a hundred men by water to Bridgnorth". This also highlights the strategic significance of the river during the War.

When the King and his army left, Ottley became Governor of the town and as the war developed he set about improving the defences to withstand a Parliamentary siege or attack. Trenches were dug around the southern and western sides of the town "from against Mr King's house in Coleham to ... the little Water Lane by Cowy's house in ye Abbey Foregate ... [and] ... a trench from ye Windmill banke at ye further end of Frankwell ... downe to Severne field".

Shrewsbury, however, was never completely secure, particularly from the furtive actions of those people in the town who opposed the King. On Saturday the 21st October there was an explosion, possibly a store of gunpowder blown up. Royalists suspected some of the inhabitants, and soldiers were heard saying that they would "hang the mayor and some of the best gents from sign posts, disarm the meaner sort of people and expel them from town".

More activity took place in the town when Prince Rupert replaced the luckless Lord Capel as Captain General of the Royalist army in the region. Rupert made his headquarters at "Master Jones" house, a notable lawyer. Today the building is the "Prince Rupert Hotel". He and his officers are said to have met at the Golden Cross Inn. The castle was effectively turned into a magazine and store to support his intended military campaign.

The town was captured by Parliament in February 1645 suspiciously easily, suggesting further treachery from within (see chapter 2). Prince Maurice had drained the garrison of men to march northwards. The Parliamentarians, seeing their chance, attacked in the early hours of the 9th February. However, it appeared that they had significant help from someone within who, it is assumed, opened one of the defensive gates. Humphrey Mackworth was subsequently appointed governor of the town. The fall of Shrewsbury was a significant blow to the Royalist war effort. It was never regained, despite some later Royalist plots that were easily uncovered.

Stoke-on-Tern

There is evidence of a Parliamentary garrison in the parish of Stoke-upon-Tern, near Market Drayton. Certainly by 1644 there are references to it by Vicars in the 'Burning Bush' and in papers relating to the Earl of Denbigh. Indeed, Denbigh's

troops occupied the area during the period in which their commander was in London fighting to retain his Commission. The most likely site of the garrison was the old moated manor house, then the seat of Sir John Corbet, formerly Sheriff of Shropshire in 1629, and a prominent supporter of Parliament. Archaeological remains of the "castle" have been recorded near to the modern manor house.

Stokesay Castle

Lawrence of Ludlow, a wealthy wool merchant, erected the fortified manor house at Stokesay, near Ludlow, sometime during 1281-1291. In 1291 he received a licence from Edward I to "crenellate" the house, that is to make a building defendable through the addition of battlements.

By the outbreak of the Civil War the castle had passed into the hands of the Craven family, but it was let on a long lease to Charles Baldwin. Baldwin had been an MP for the town of Ludlow. Both he and Lord Craven were supporters of Charles I and the castle was soon garrisoned for the King. A Captain Daurett was appointed governor and appears to have remained in command until it was taken by Parliament at the beginning of June 1645. The mercenary Reinking had prepared his army for a siege and called upon the garrison to surrender, which they refused to do, but "being ready to fall on, gave a second summons, ... a parley admitted, and the castle delivered up".

Once taken, the castle had to be defended. Around June 8th, Sir Michael Woodhouse amassed around two thousand troops, in an attempt to re-take it. However, the Royalists were stopped at Wistanstow where they were severely defeated, losing over one hundred men. (see Wistanstow).

Soldiers may well have damaged Stokesay Church in order to prevent the enemy gaining a firing point close to the Castle. There is little evidence to suggest that it was attacked during a later skirmish in 1646, as some stories imply.

Tong Castle

By 1642, the ancient castle at Tong, near Shifnal, was owned by William Pierpoint, the second son of the Earl of Kingston. Pierpoint was an MP for Much Wenlock during the Long Parliament and an opponent of the King. In November 1644 he played an important role as one of the Parliamentary Commissioners entreating with the King.

Often known as "wise William", he became a close friend of Cromwell.

Located on the Shropshire-Staffordshire border, Tong Castle changed hands many times during the war. Parliament sought to occupy it towards the end of 1643, but Francis Ottley learned of the design and quickly garrisoned it for the King. On the 28th of December, Parliamentary forces under Captain Stone of Eccleshall fell upon a Royalist party who had vacated the castle for an expedition. Some were killed and two hundred taken prisoner. Tong remained under Parliamentary control until April 1644. Its fall coincided with the return of Prince Rupert to Shropshire, who re-asserted the King's authority. Despite efforts to raise assistance from Staffordshire and the Earl of Denbigh, the castle surrendered to Colonel Tyllier after a siege lasting two weeks. However, once Parliament had established control over most of Shropshire in 1646, many outposts including Tong were deserted.

The church at Tong was also affected by the wars. A soldier, Richard Symonds, noted that it was a "faire church" but "the windows much broken". There is also some evidence of bullet marks and cannon shot on the North side of the church, as a result of fighting in or around it.

Wellington

Wellington remained relatively unscathed during the war. Apley Castle (qv), to the north-east of the town, provided the most significant objective for both the Royalists and Parliament. The King slept at Wellington on the 19th September 1642, en-route from Nottingham to Shrewsbury. At this time he possessed only about four thousand horse and a smaller number of foot. His support had not been consolidated. In an effort to dispel fear and propaganda from Parliament, Charles rallied his troops. Making a speech while standing amongst them he said:

> "Your consciences and your loyalty have brought you hither to fight for your religion, your King, and the laws of the land. You shall meet with no enemies but traitors, most of them Brownists, Anabaptists and Atheists, such who desire to destroy both Church and State, and who have already condemned you to ruin for being loyal to us".

Later, the King was greeted by Sir John Weld, Sheriff of Shropshire, who was to escort His Majesty to Shrewsbury. The Mayor of that town was also present in the Sheriff's party. Significantly, he failed to deliver a written speech in which the people of Shrewsbury called for a re-union of "these disjointed governments". The King left Wellington and arrived to a seemingly joyous and loyal reception at Shrewsbury.

For a short time the church was garrisoned by Parliament, but was evacuated when Apley Castle fell to the Royalists in March 1644. Soldiers passed through the town on numerous occasions, but there is little or no evidence of fighting. Upon the Wrekin, which overlooks Wellington, folklore maintains that the place-names "Heaven's Gate" and "Hell's Gate" are derived from the Civil War skirmishes in which, of course, Cromwell is usually involved. Anyone ascending the hill today will quickly realise the improbability of this notion, particularly as Cromwell never visited Shropshire during the wars.

Wem

At the outbreak of war Wem did not declare for one side or the other. Part of the King's army had stayed in the town around September or October 1642, but did not remain or fortify it. It was not until one year later when the Parliamentary forces were sufficiently organised to push into north Shropshire from Cheshire that a garrison was placed in Wem. In September 1643 an army led by Brereton, Middleton and Mytton, seized the town without opposition. Archaeological evidence shows that a ditch about four yards wide with a rampart, starting and finishing at Drayton Gate was erected around the town to fortify it. The buildings immediately outside the town were razed to the ground so that they would not become shelters for any attackers. An outpost of the garrison was established in Loppington (qv). The arrival of Richard Baxter, the Puritan divine, and his followers further strengthened support for the garrison.

Lord Capel quickly attempted to regain the town for the King on 17th October 1643. Although a much smaller force, the Parliamentarian garrison defeated the Royalists, much to the embarrassment of Capel (see Chapter 2 and Lord Capel).

A plan of Wem from a seventeenth century estate map. Note that north and south are transposed.

The Battle of Wem, re-enacted by the Civil War Society

Gateway. Council House

The Council House, Shrewsbury, host to Charles I in 1642 and formerly a temporary residence for the Council of the Marches

Golden Cross Passage, Shrewsbury: Location for an early Baptist meeting house.
Royalist officers also met in the local inn.

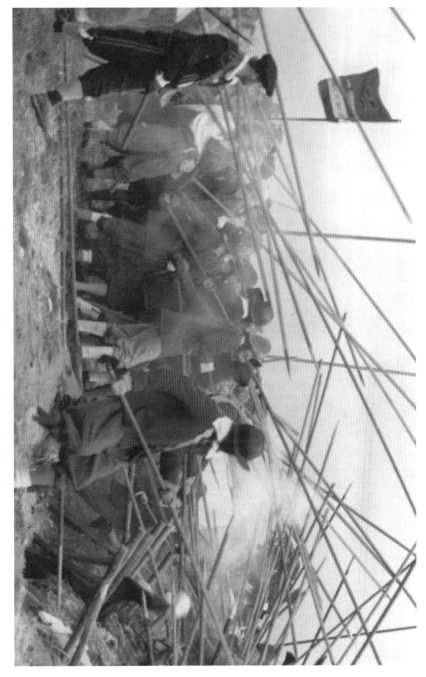

Early skirmishes in the Battle of Wem, re-enacted by the Civil War Society

Stokesay Castle managed to escape serious damage in the wars, despite its being garrisoned by both sides. Today it is open to visitors.

Major's Leap on Wenlock Edge is enshrined in Civil War folk-lore after the deeds of Thomas Smallman.

Wilderhope Manor, seventeenth century home of the Royalist Thomas Smallman, now a youth hostel owned by the YHA.

The Parliamentary Committee for Shropshire had little alternative than to make Wem their headquarters and they remained there throughout most of the war. In 1644 the Royalist army made a concerted effort to take Wem, which was still the main Parliamentarian stronghold in the County. However, Prince Rupert declined to lay siege to the town calling it "a crow's nest that would not afford each of his men a piece of bread". Instead, it was left to Lord Byron and his Irish soldiers to attack the town in April the same year. The town's situation became desperate as Byron laid siege to it throughout the month. Provisions could not be brought into the town and there was only enough food for two weeks. By the end of the month the garrison thought it could survive little more than ten days, but Byron did not have intelligence of this and the siege was abandoned. Had Wem fallen, Parliament's position within the county would have become extremely perilous. The failure of Byron to take Wem, or of Rupert to recognise its importance to Parliament's cause in the region, allowed the Parliamentary Committee for Shropshire to pursue the enemy with renewed vigour.

The Royalists made a further attempt on Wem in May 1645, when the King was in Shropshire. He ordered Sir Marmaduke Langdale to surprise the town in the knowledge that the garrison numbered only a hundred and fifty or so soldiers. Again, the plan did not succeed as Langdale arrived too late, leaving Parliament time to re-group.

Despite some Royalist sentiment within the town, Wem remained a stronghold for Parliament until the end of the wars.

Whitchurch

Whitchurch prospered during the early seventeenth century. Mercers like Thomas Eddoes were selling spices, luxury fabrics, tobacco and books.
The town's high street began to specialise when oats were sold at the northern end of the street; hemp, linseed and rye near Pepper Street; French wheat, peas, beans and vetches between Pepper Street and the Old Crown. Tanners sold their wares between the Red Lion and St Mary's Street and shoemakers were located in the Bull Ring. Its population had risen from around eight hundred in the early sixteenth century to about three thousand in 1640.

At the outbreak of war, Whitchurch was reported to have been "enthusiastically Royalist". Sir William Brereton, the local Parliamentarian commander considered it to be a "malignant place" and Charles I passed through the town en-route to Chester in order to raise his army and money for it in late 1642. The town did not see serious fighting until 1643, when Brereton, having intercepted a letter, realised that Capel had left the town poorly defended. He captured the town on 30th May, killing a hundred and fifty Royalists and taking £2,000 that had been in the charge of Sir Michael Woodhouse. Capel was forced to withdraw to Shrewsbury, but Whitchurch was not held as a garrison by Parliament because it did not have a castle or other structures that afforded good fortification. It would have required funds and manpower to hold it. Furthermore, it was close to both Nantwich and Wem, which were considered to be more important. However Parliament continued to control the town by moving its troops in and using it strategically when required. On 18th March 1645, Major Braine advised Brereton that Whitchurch was a "good place ... to engage the enemy", yet it was also quite possible for opposing troops to move around the vicinity of the town unmolested. This situation appeared to continue until Parliament finally secured the county in 1646.

Wilderhope Manor

Wilderhope is an early seventeenth century manor house near Wenlock Edge, two miles south of Longville. Its connection with the Civil War is through the curious stories relating to one Major Thomas Smallman, a zealous Royalist and heir to the Wilderhope estate. It is alleged that one day during the wars he returned home to discover that some Parliamentary troops had visited Wilderhope and looted some items. Angered by his loss of property, Smallman decided to ambush the looters on the road to Ludlow, and is said to have killed two or three of the troopers in the recovery of his stolen goods.

The same man was involved in a legendary escape when chased by Parliamentary troops. With the enemy gaining on him, he became trapped at the top of Wenlock Edge - a steep limestone escarpment with sheer drops to the fields below.

In desperation he plunged his horse over the side. Smallman apparently survived this desperate act, although his poor horse died. The Parliamentarians sensibly declined to follow. The point at which Smallman supposedly rode over the cliff is known locally as Major's or Smallman's Leap, and is a popular viewing spot for visitors to the Edge. Whether the tale is true or not, it is certainly a romantic story of the 'dashing Cavalier' genre.

Wistanstow

After Parliament had taken Stokesay (qv) at the beginning of June 1645, Sir Michael Woodhouse, the Governor of Ludlow, quickly attempted its recapture. He summoned around two thousand men and marched to the castle via Broncroft. Parliamentary forces in the vicinity retreated to Wistanstow, but with little prospect of reinforcements they were compelled to take on the larger Royalist army. A short brutal engagement near Wistanstow followed. The Parliamentarian Kingdom's Weekly Intelligencer reported:

"Captain Fouke's troope with some reformadoes fell upon a body of 200 of the enemies' horse, and routed them; after whom our foot marched, beate up their ambuscades for a mile together till they came to the maine body, which after an hour's fight were routed and dispersed."

A hundred Royalists were killed and three hundred soldiers taken prisoner.

Wroxeter

The church at Wroxeter is of interest because it contains an altar rail that is dated 1637. This is an example of Archbishop Laud's reforms, which were so hated by the Puritans, as they feared this represented a return towards Catholicism. Few such altar rails survived as the Parliamentarian army removed many. It is more remarkable as Wroxeter was held by Parliament at various times during the war. The village was also a point of rendezvous for the forces of the Earl of Denbigh, en-route to Oswestry.

Suggested Further Reading

Acton, Frances Stackhouse   The Garrisons of Shropshire during the Civil War, 1642-48; 1867.

Archdeaconary of Ludlow Acts of Office, HRO.

Aubrey, John Brief lives (ed. Oliver Lawson Dick, 1949).

Auden, Alfred M. Clun and its neighbourhood in the first Civil War; Transactions of the Shropshire Archaeological and Historical Society, 3rd ser., vol. 8.

Auden, H.M. The Penderel annuities in 1665; Transactions of the Shropshire Archaeological and Historical Society, 4th ser., vol. 7.

Auden Rev. J.E.   Articles in Transactions of the Shropshire Archaeological and Historical Society, 3rd ser., vols. 7, 8, 10, 50; 4th ser., vols. 2, 7, 47, 51.

Auden, Rev. Thomas   Sidelights of the Civil War from some old parish registers of Shropshire; Antiquary, July 1902.

Baugh G.C. (ed.)   A history of Shropshire; Victoria County History, vol. 3, 1979.

Baugh G.C. (ed.)   A history of Shropshire; Victoria County History, vol. 4, 1989.

Beaumont, H. Arthur, Lord Capel, the King's Lieutenant General for Shropshire; Transactions of the Shropshire Archaeological and Historical Society, vol. 50.

Beaumont, H. Events in Shropshire at the commencement of the Civil War; Transactions of the Shropshire Archaeological and Historical Society; vol. 51.

Beaumont, H.   Shrewsbury and Ship Money; Transactions of the Shropshire Archaeological and Historical Society, vol. 49.

Bellett, Rev. G.   The antiquities of Bridgnorth, with some historical notices of the town and castle; 1856.

Blakeway, J.B.   History of Shrewsbury Hundred or Liberties; (Rev W.G.D. Fletcher ed.), reprinted from Transactions of the Shropshire Archaeological and Historical Society, 1897.

Blount, H.   Boscobel: or the history of His Sacred Majesties most miraculous preservation after the battle of Worcester. 3. Sept. 1651; 1660.

Bryan, T   "For King or Parliament": An English Civil War trail through south-west Shropshire.

Calamy, R.   Abridgement of Mr. Baxter's History of his life and times ...; 1713.

Calendar of state papers. Domestic series, 1641-1649; 1649-1651; HMSO; 1877-

Camden, William   Britannia, 1610.

Champion, [W.A.] Bill Everyday life in Tudor Shrewsbury; 1994.

Champion, W.A.   The economy of Shrewsbury 1400-1560/1660; MS SRR 6001/6866; 1987.

Champion, W.A.   Population change in Shrewsbury, 1400-1700; MS SRR 6001/6821; 1983.

Chapels and dissenting places of worship; Salopian Magazine, Oct. 31, no.10, 1815.

Clarendon, Edward Hyde Earl of,   The history of the rebellion; 1717 edn.

Condren, C.   George Lawson's 'Politica' and the English Revolution; 1989.

Condren, C (ed.)   Lawson: Politica sacra et civilis; Cambridge texts in the history of political thought; 1993.

Corbet, A.E.   The Family of Corbet, its life and times; 1915.

Cranage, D.H.S.   An architectural account of the churches of Shropshire; 1901.

Defoe, D.   Memoirs of a cavalier in England: Memoirs of the Honourable Col. Andrew Newport, a Shropshire gentleman, who served as a cavalier in the army of Gustavus Adolphus in Germany and in that of Charles The First in England; 1792. [Note: This is probably a fictitious account by Defoe. See essay on Newport Family in main text.]

Diocese of Hereford, Stottesden Deanery Acts of Office (transcribed by H. Oliver).

Dore, R.N. (ed.)   The letter books of Sir William Brereton; Record society of Lancashire and Cheshire, 1984-90.

Duggan, T.C.   The history of Whitchurch, Shropshire; 1935.

Eales, Jacqueline   Puritans and Roundheads. The Harleys of Brampton Bryan and the outbreak of the English Civil War; 1990.

Edwards, P R. The farming economy of north-east Shropshire in the seventeenth century; D.Phil. thesis, Oxford, 1976.

Farraday, M.   Ludlow 1085-1660: A social, economic and political history; 1992.

Farrow, W.J.   The Great Civil War in Shropshire, 1642-49; 1929.

Forrest, H.E.   The old houses of Shrewsbury; 1911.

Francis-Wemyss, Peter   Sir Vincent Corbet's Dragoons; Intelligencer, Journal of Tudor and Stuart Life, vol. 1, no.1, August 1993.

Garbett, Rev. S.   The history of Wem; 1818.

Garner, L.   Churches of Shropshire, 1994.

Gilbert, C.D. Clubmen in South West Shropshire 1644-45; Transactions of the Shropshire Archaeological and Historical Society; vol. 68.

Gough, Richard   Antiquities and memorials of the parish of Myddle; 1701.

Herbert, E   The autobiography of Edward, Lord Herbert of Chirbury; (ed. W.R. Dicks); 1888.

Herbert, E   The life of Edward, Lord Herbert of Cherbury, written by himself; 1770.

Historic Manuscripts Commission, The manuscripts of the Earl of Rt. Hon. The Earl of Denbigh; HMC 4th Report, 1874.

Historic Manuscripts Commission, The manuscripts of the Corporation of Bridgnorth and the Rev. J. Walcot; HMC 10th report, 1885.

Hopkins, Eric   The Bridgewater estates

in North Shropshire during the civil war; Transactions of the Shropshire Archaeological and Historical Society, vol. 56.

Hopkins, Eric   The Bridgewater estates in North Shropshire in the first half of the seventeenth century; MA Thesis, Univeristy of London, 1953.

Hutton, R. The Royalist war effort; 1982.

Jones, L (ed.)   Churchwardens' Accounts of the town of Ludlow; reprinted from the Transactions of the Shropshire Archaeological and Historical Society, 1889-93.

Journals of the House of Commons; vols. 3-6, 1642-51.

Journals of the House of Lords; vols. 5-9, 1642-47.

Kenyon, R. L.   Committee for the sequestration of the estates of Shropshire delinquents; reprinted from Transactions of the Shropshire Archaeological and Historical Society, 1894.

Kenyon, R. L.   History of the Shrewsbury Mint; Transactions of the Shropshire Archaeological and Historical Society, 2nd ser., vol. 10.

Kingston, H.P.   The wanderings of Charles II in Staffordshire and Shropshire after the Worcester fight, September 3rd, 1651; 1933.

Lake, Peter   Puritanism, Arminianism and a Shropshire axe-murder; Midland History, vol. 15, 1990.

Leach, F.   County seats of Shropshire; 1891.

Leighton, Stanley (ed.)   Mytton manuscripts. Letters and papers of Thomas Mytton of Halston; Montgomeryshire Collections, vol. 7 & 8, 1875-6.

Malbon, T.   Memorials of the Civil War in Cheshire and the adjacent counties; Lancashire & Cheshire Record Society, 1889.

Martin, Evelyn H.   Bromcroft in the parish of Diddlebury, and its owners; Transactions of the Shropshire Archaeological and Historical Society, 4th ser., vol. 6.

Mendenhall, T.C. Social status of prominent Shrewsbury Drapers; Transactions of the Shropshire Archaeological and Historical Society, vol. 54.

Nussey, John   The Will of Trooper Oldroyd of Heckmondwicke - an incident in the Civil War; Yorkshire Archaeological Journal, vol. 59, 1987.

O'Riordan, C. Sequestration and social upheaval: Madeley, Shropshire and the English Revolution; West Midlands Studies, vol. 18, winter, 1985.

Omerod, J. The history of the county palatine and city of Chester; 1819.

Owen H. & Blakeway J.B.   A history of Shrewsbury; 1825.

Pepys, S.   An account of His Majesty's escape from Worcester, dictated to Mr. Pepys by the King himself; 1680.

Phillips, J.R. Memoirs of the Civil War in Wales and the Marches 1642-49; 1878.

Phillips, T   A history of Shrewsbury, 1779.

Phillips, W.   Mss. Relating to the Civil War; SRR 6001/235.

Phillips, W.   Shropshire Men; MS vols. SRR.

Phillips, W. (ed.)   The Ottley papers relating to the Civil War; 1893.

Pigott, Harriet   Collections for the life of Thomas Mytton; Pigott MS, Bodleian Library.

Sessions, William K.   A world of mischiefe: The King's Printer in York in 1642 and in Shrewsbury 1642-43; 1981.

Sessions, William K.   The King's Printer in Shrewsbury, 1642-1643; 1979.

Skeel, Caroline A.J.   The Council in the Marches of Wales; 1904.

Skinner, R.F.   Nonconformity in Shropshire 1662-1816; 1964.

Somerset, J.A.B. (ed.)   Records of early English drama, Shropshire; 1994.

Speed, John   England, Wales, Scotland and Ireland described; 1612.

Stamper, Paul   Farmer feeds us all: a short history of Shropshire agriculture; 1989.

Symonds, Richard   Diary of the marches of the Royal Army during the Great Civil War; Camden Society, 1879.

Three Mytton letters; Transactions of the Shropshire Archaeological and Historical Society, 3rd ser., vol. 9.

Tucker, Norman   North Wales in the Civil War; 1958.

Vicars, John   England's worthies, under whom all the civill and bloudy warres since 1642 to 1647, are related; 1647.

Walker, John   The sufferings of the clergy; 1714.

Wanklyn M.D.G. and Young, P.   A King in search of soldiers: Charles I in 1642. A rejoinder; The Historical Journal, vol. 24, no. 1, 1981.

Wanklyn, M.D.G.   Landownership, political authority and social status in Shropshire and Cheshire 1500-1700; West Midlands Studies, vol. 11, 1978.

Wanklyn, M.D.G.   Recusancy in seventeenth century Shropshire, with particular reference to the parish of Madeley; Worcestershire Recusant, June 1984.

Wanklyn, M.D.G.   The Severn navigation in the seventeenth century: Long-distance trade of Shrewsbury Boats, Midland History, vol. 13, 1988.

Wanklyn, M.D.G.   Shropshire recusants in 1635; Midland Catholic History, no. 3, 1994.

Wanklyn, M.D.G.   Urban revival in early modern England: Bridgnorth and the river trade, 1660-1800; Midland History, vol. 18, 1993.

Watts, Sylvia   Evidence for population growth and economic prosperity in Whitchurch in the sixteenth and seventeenth centuries; Whitchurch Archaeological Group, Newsletter no. 52, 1993.

Watts, Sylvia   The small market town in the large multi-township parish: Shifnal, Wellington, Wem and Whitchurch c.1535-c.1660; PhD. Thesis, University of Wolverhampton, 1995.

Weyman H.T.   The MP's for Shropshire; reprinted from the Transactions of the Shropshire Archaeological and Historical Society, 1925-30.

Whitlocke, B   Memorials of the English affairs; 1682.

Williams, Penry   The activity of the Council of the Marches under the early Stuarts; Welsh History Review, vol. 1, no. 2, 1961.

Civil War Tracts, Sermons, etc.

A copy of a letter sent from Sir Tho. Middleton, to the Honorable, William Lenthall Esq; Speaker of the House of Commons. Concerning the raising of the siege at Oswestree, July 3. 1644.

A militarie sermon wherein by the word of God, the nature and disposition of a rebell is discovered, and the King's true souldier described and characterised: preached at Shrewsbury, May 19, 1644 ... by Edw. Symmons.

A more exact particular relation of the taking of Shrewsbury then hath hitherto been published. With the manner and performance thereof by Lieutenant, Collonel William Reinking, commander in chief in that design.

An address to the people of Shropshire on the occasion of the present rebellion; n.d. c.1642.

An ordinance of the Lords and Commons assembled in Parliament for the raising of monies for the maintenance of such forces are and shall be raised for the service of parliament; 1644.

Arthur Lord Capell Lieutenant Generall under the Prince His Highnesse of His Majesties Forces, in the Counties of Worcester, Salop, and Chester ... To all Commanders, Officers, and Souldiers, and to all other His Majesties subjects ..., printed at Shrewsbury by Robert Barker, 1643; King's Printers Catalogue No. 126, British Library.

His Majesty's declaration to all his soldiers ...' also his speech and protestation, made in the head of his Army, between Stafford and Wellington; 1642.

Intelligence from Shropshire of three great victories obtained by the forces of Shrewsbury, viz. The taking of Stokesay and Cause – castles; 1645.

Mercurius Aulicus, communicating the intelligence and affaires of the Court, to the rest of the Kingdome. From July 13. To July 20. 1645.

Resolution of the Clergy of the county of Salop to associate ye high sheriffe. The Commissioners for ye Army, the Gentry, freeholders and others of the said County, rsponsive to their resolution, August 24, 1642. (Copy) SRR 6000/15360.

The copy of a letter of the taking of High-Archall, 27th March 1646; Hereford & Worcester Record Office, 899 : 31 BA3669/1 xxviii.

The relation of the manner of the taking of Shrewsbury on Saturday the 22th of February, 1644 [1645] by Collonel Mittton and Collonel Bowyer.

The saints gain by death and their assurance thereof. A sermon preached at the funeral of that worthy patriot, Richard More ... by Humphrey Hardwick; 1644.

The souldiers catechisme composed for the Parliaments Army; 1644.

Two great victories obtained by the Earle of Denbigh at Oswestry; 1644.

Two petitions. The one presented to the Honourable house of Commons, from the Countie of Hereford, May the fourth, 1642. The other, to his Majestie, and the Parliament, from the Towne of Ludlow in the countie of Salop. 1642.

Civil War and seventeenth century documents etc., Shropshire Records & Research Centre

SRR 103/1/10/54
SRR 212/ Box 364/65
SRR 224/2
SRR 228/3
SRR 366/1
SRR 445/2846
SRR 3217/97
SRR 3365/224-25, 589, 2240, 2570-72
SRR 4122/7/7
SRR 4597/17
SRR 4630/11
SRR 5110/11/6
SRR 5460/8/2/2
SRR 6000/ 2361, 4233, 8893, 13284-13319, 13528, 16149, 17047, 17050, 18146
SRR DA2/4001 box 22
SRR LB 7/1931-32, 2183-84, 2249-51, 2315-20
SRR LB 8/3/75-76
SRR LB11/4/76
SRR LB14/792-832, 851-887

Subject Index

Name Index

Place Index

More Books on Shropshire's History published by Shropshire Books

EVERYDAY LIFE IN TUDOR SHREWSBURY
Bill Champion

£7.95

EVERYDAY LIFE IN MEDIEVAL SHREWSBURY
Dorothy Cromarty

£7.95

SHREWSBURY ABBEY - A Medieval Monastery
Nigel Baker

£6.95

SHREWSBURY THEN AND NOW

£5.50

SHROPSHIRE FROM THE AIR - Man and the Landscape
Michael Watson and Chris Musson

£13.99

SHROPSHIRE FROM THE AIR - An English County at Work
Michael Watson and Chris Musson

£12.99

BLUE RIBBON DAYS - A Tale of Victorian Childhood,
Love and Marriage in Shropshire, by Thomas Lewis

£5.99

PREHISTORIC, ROMAN, ANGLO-SAXON, NORMAN
And MEDIEVAL SHROPSHIRE - A series of pictorial leaflets
on Shropshire Archaeology which fold out into posters

£1.25 each

For a complete list of Shropshire Books titles contact:

Shropshire Books
Column House
7 London Road
SHREWSBURY SY2 6NW
Tel: (01743) 255043
Fax: (01743) 255050

or visit our website on **www.shropshirebooks.co.uk**